POWER FOR POSITIVE LIVING

JOY OF LIVING BIBLE STUDY SERIES

POWER FOR POSITIVE LIVING

Studies in Philippians and Colossians

Life-Related for Personal and Group Study
DORIS W. GREIG

Regal Books
A Division of GL Publications
Ventura, California, U.S.A.

Published by Regal Books
A Division of GL Publications
Ventura, California 93006
Printed in U.S.A.

Scripture quotations used in this publication are taken from:

Beck—*The New Testament in the Language of Today,* by William F. Beck, © Copyright 1963 by Concordia Publishing House, St. Louis, Missouri.
JB—Jerusalem Bible, © 1966 by Darton, Longman and Todd, Ltd. and Doubleday and Co., Inc.
KJV—*King James Version.*
NASB—*New American Standard Bible.* © The Lockman Foundation 1960, 1962, 1963, 1968, 1971, 1972, 1973, 1975. Used by permission.
NEB—From *The New English Bible.* © The Delegates of the Oxford University Press and The Syndics of the Cambridge University Press 1961, 1970. Reprinted by permission.
NIV—Scripture taken from the HOLY BIBLE: NEW INTERNATIONAL VERSION. Copyright © 1973, 1978, 1984 by the International Bible Society. Used by permission of Zondervan Bible Publishers.
Phillips—THE NEW TESTAMENT IN MODERN ENGLISH, Revised edition, J.B. Phillips, Translator. © J.B. Phillips 1958, 1960, 1972. Used by permission of Macmillan Publishing Co., Inc.
RSV—*Revised Standard Version.* From *RSV* of the Bible, copyrighted 1946 and 1952 by the Division of Christian Education of the NCCC, U.S.A., and used by permission.
TLB—From *The Living Bible,* Copyright © 1971 by Tyndale House Publishers, Wheaton, Illinois. Used by permission.

© Copyright 1988 by Joy of Living Bible Studies
All rights reserved.

Any omission of credits or permissions granted is unintentional. The publisher requests documentation for future printings.

Library of Congress Cataloging-in-Publication Data:
Greig, Doris W.
   Power for positive living : studies in Philippians and Colossians / by Doris W. Greig.
   p.   cm.
ISBN 0-8307-1286-0
   1. Bible. N.T. Philippians—Study. 2. Bible. N.T. Colossians—Study. I. Title.
BS2705.5.C74   1988
227'.6'0076-dc19   88-4628
                                                                                   CIP

2 3 4 5 6 7 8 9 10 / 91 90 89 88

Rights for publishing this book in other languages are contracted by Gospel Literature International (GLINT) foundation. GLINT also provides technical help for the adaptation, translation, and publishing of Bible study resources and books in scores of languages worldwide. For further information, contact GLINT, Post Office Box 488, Rosemead, California, 91770, U.S.A., or the publisher.

SPECIAL BENEFIT

This book has been conveniently hole-punched and perforated for easy tearout and insertion in a 6" × 9½" looseleaf notebook:

- Bible study pages lie flat in your notebook for ease of writing as you study.
- Additional notebook paper can be inserted for journaling or more extensive notes and other relevant information.
- Additonal studies in the Joy of Living Series can be inserted, along with your personal notes, and tabbed to help you build your Bible study file for easy, future reference.

CONTENTS

Introduction   9

How to Use this Book   11

PART I   PHILIPPIANS

1. Jesus Christ—Our Joy and Hope   15
Inexpressible joy comes in knowing God has a plan for your life.

2. United in Love   33
Christians are called to be united in love with a common purpose and like-mindedness.

3. Rejoice in the Lord!   49
Christians can be joyful, even in a world full of sorrow.

4. Stand Fast in the Knowledge of Christ   67
It is only by standing fast in Jesus Christ that Christians can resist temptation and live victorious lives.

PART II   COLOSSIANS

5. The Supreme Lordship of Jesus Christ   87
Christians need to examine their beliefs and put Christ Jesus in His rightful place.

6. Grow in His Wisdom and Knowledge   103
The best way to be protected from the world is to have an understanding of Christ's perfection.

7. Christ Is All-sufficient   121
To find real and satisfying life, focus in on the all-sufficiency of Jesus Christ.

8. Christians and Their World   137
Christ is seen and felt by those around us every day as we live out our Christianity.

INTRODUCTION

Many health-conscious people are walking several miles each day at a rapid pace in order to have healthy muscles and organs. Yet, how many think of spending time walking with God for a certain amount of time each day for the sake of a healthy spirit? It is important to seek power for positive living by reading the Bible, God's message to us. In a sense we can say that this is where we get our spiritual vitamins for each day.

God's instructions for the necessity of a daily walk in His Word are found throughout the Scriptures. God led the apostle Paul to write these words in Ephesians: "Finally, be strong in the Lord, and in the strength of His might" (6:10, *NASB*). We need a daily walk with Christ Jesus in order for Him to impart such strength to us, which in turn will give us power for positive living.

As you study the Epistles of Philippians and Colossians, you will learn how to walk in the Lord's power. The Holy Spirit led Paul to write some wonderful truths about faith and how to live a life filled with power for positive living in these letters. There are timeless principles, which when exercised in faith will help you to experience Jesus Christ's power and guidance for each day. In faith you can thank God for "Him who is able to do exceeding abundantly beyond all that we ask or think, according to the power that works within us, to Him *be* the glory in the church and in Christ Jesus to all generations forever and ever. Amen" (Eph. 3:20,21, *NASB*).

Further, you will find God's grace, peace and spiritual blessings (Eph. 1:2,3), plus many other promises of God's power for your life. These Bible truths are essential for all Christians who hope to live a victorious life amid life's stresses and strains. The Lord led Paul to write the words: "I consider my life worth nothing to me, if only I may finish the race and complete the task the Lord Jesus has given me" (Acts 20:24, *NIV*). What a great goal Paul had for his life! Let's join him in the race, as we find power for positive living in God's Word!

HOW TO USE THIS BOOK

The Bible is a living book! It is relevant and powerful, but more than that, it is the active voice of our living God, and He wants to communicate with you daily through His Word. As you study the Bible, you will learn about God's person and character. You will begin to find His purpose for your life as He speaks to you through His written Word. His purpose is unchanging and His principles are unfailing guidelines for living. He will show you His truth and what your response should be to it.

Will you set aside a special time each day to interact with God in His Word? As you read, study, meditate and memorize His Word, the Holy Spirit will guide you, and His direction for your life will be made clear. More and more, His voice will be easily discerned in the din of life's pressures. When your heart is available and you see God's good intentions for you, you will then learn how to respond to the Lord's individual call to you day by day, moment by moment. As you train your ears to hear the voice of God, you will recognize His presence in the most unlikely circumstances and places. "The grass withers and the flowers fall, but the word of our God stands forever" (Isa. 40:8, *NIV*).

Will you choose to hear from God today? Open your Bible and turn to the study questions in Lesson 1. It is good to read the passage in several versions of the Bible, if you have them available. Each version may add new insights. Try not to use a commentary or any other reference book until you have allowed the Lord to personally speak to you from His word.

At the beginning of each set of questions, you will find suggestions for getting the most from your study of God's Word.

There are six sections of questions in each lesson. You will find it most beneficial to do one section daily. This will allow you time to meditate on God's Word and really hear what He has to say to you personally. When you have completed the questions, carefully read the study notes, which follow, and look up the Scripture verses. This will give you added insight on the lesson you have just completed.

This study is designed to be used individually or in a group. If you're studying in a group, we urge you to actively share your answers and thoughts. In sharing we give encouragement to others and learn from one another.

May God bless you as you begin your journey into His Word. This may be the first time for you to take this trip, or it may be that you have journeyed this way many times before. No matter what trip it is for you, we pray you will find new joy and hope as you seek to live in the light of the living God!

PART 1
PHILIPPIANS

1. Jesus Christ—Our Joy and Hope
2. United in Love
3. Rejoice in the Lord!
4. Stand Fast in the Knowledge of Christ

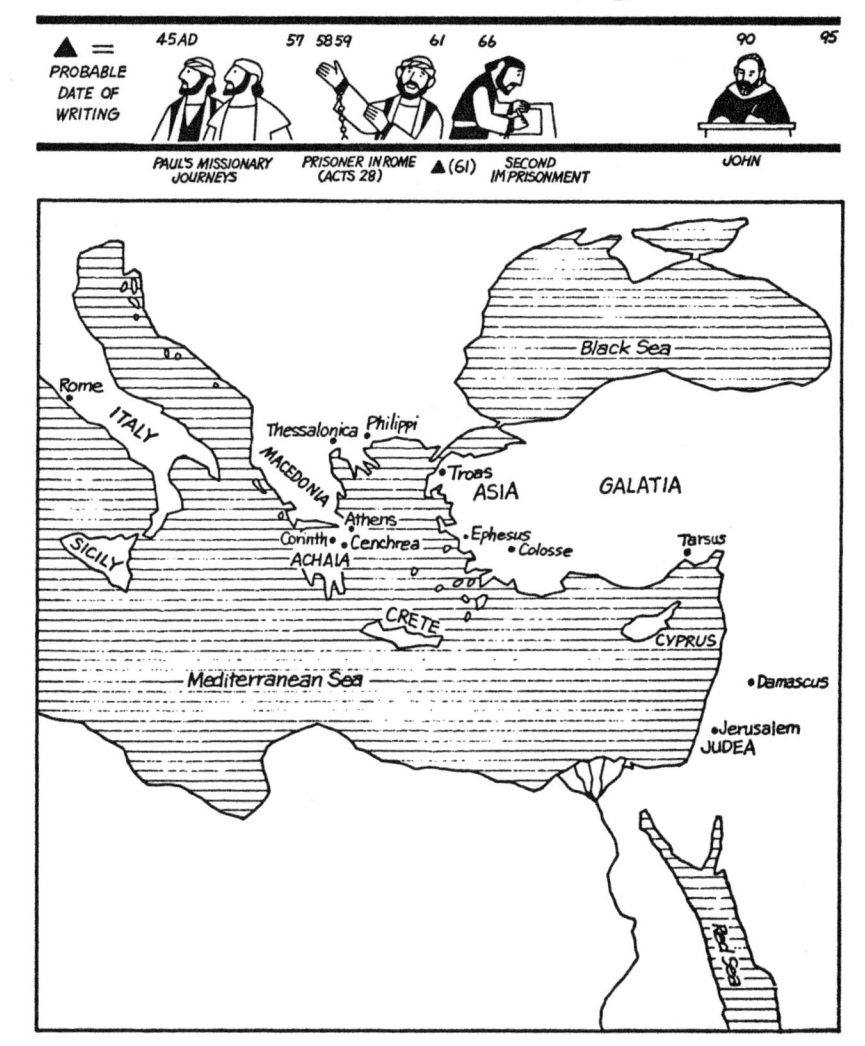

▲ = PROBABLE DATE OF WRITING

| 45 AD | 57 58 59 | 61 | 66 | 90 | 95 |

PAUL'S MISSIONARY JOURNEYS | PRISONER IN ROME (ACTS 28) | ▲(61) SECOND IMPRISONMENT | JOHN

PART 1

PHILIPPIANS

1. Jesus Christ—Our Joy and Hope
2. United in Love
3. Rejoice in the Lord!
4. Stand Fast in the Knowledge of Christ

JESUS CHRIST—
OUR JOY AND HOPE
PHILIPPIANS 1

Before you begin your study this week:
1. Pray and ask God to speak to you through His Holy Spirit each day.
2. Use only your Bible for your answers.
3. Write your answers and the verses you have used.
4. Challenge questions are for those who have the time and wish to do them.
5. Personal questions are to be shared with your study group only if you wish to share.
6. As you study look for a verse to memorize this week. Write it down, carry it with you, tack it to your bulletin board, tape it to the dashboard of your car. Make a real effort to learn the verse and its reference.

FIRST DAY: Read Philippians 1 concentrating on verses 1-6.

1. What does Paul call Timothy and himself in this chapter? To whom is Paul writing this letter?

2. **Challenge:** If you are a believer in Jesus Christ and trust Him as your Savior and Lord, then you are a saint, and should be eager to be a servant for Jesus Christ. Read the following verses and state briefly what they say. How do you feel Christ might challenge and ask you to serve in some similar ways today?

Proverbs 31:20

1 Corinthians 4:2

2 Corinthians 6:3

1 Timothy 5:18

3 a. In Phillipians 1:2 we discover that God our Father and the Lord Jesus Christ give grace and peace to the Christian. Look up these words in the dictionary and put down what you think they mean from the Christian viewpoint.

Grace

Peace

b. (Personal) Have you allowed God through your faith in His Son, Jesus Christ, to give you these qualities of peace and grace spoken of in Philippians 1:2? If not, read 1 John 4:9,10 with Revelation 3:20 and act upon these verses by praying to receive Jesus Christ as your Savior and Lord.

4 a. Read Philippians 1:3-5. Think of some special Christians whom God has sent into your life. Do you do as Paul did for his Christian friends in Philippi? List the things he said he did in verses 3-5.

b. (Personal) Think of one or several people to whom you would like to show the concern Paul showed for his Christian friends. List the names of these people and pray, asking God to help you show a similar concern to them.

c. **Challenge:** Why not take time to write a letter to each one of the people you listed, sharing your love for them and your prayers and thanksgiving for what they mean to you. Perhaps you could plan to write one letter a day.

5. If you have not started a prayer notebook, perhaps this is the day to begin, by listing praise to God, prayer requests for your family and friends, national leaders, your church and yourself. If you have found a successful method for keeping a prayer record, please share this with your group.

6. What does Philippians 1:6 mean to you? How does it tie in with Romans 8:26 and Ephesians 3:16?

    Romans 8:26

    Ephesians 3:16

    Philippians 1:6

SECOND DAY: Read Philippians 1:7-14.

1. Even though Paul was chained and imprisoned, where did he carry his friends in Christ?

17

2. Paul prayed that the love of his Christian friends would abound more and more in wisdom and knowledge (see Phil 1:9). Look up wisdom and knowledge in the dictionary. Then write down what these words mean to you from the Christian perspective of love.

   Wisdom

   Knowledge

3. **Challenge:** How do you believe a Christian can grow and abound more and more in Christian wisdom and knowledge? The following verses will help you understand how the Lord will do this for a Christian. Summarize each passage.

   John 16:7-14

   Luke 6:46-48

   Proverbs 28:5

4 a. Why is wisdom so important a part of Christian love? (see Eccles. 10:12).

   b. (Personal) Can you remember a time when God gave you or someone else gracious words and you were aware that God's Holy Spirit gave them, rather than human intelligence and reasoning? Please share if possible.

5 a. What does 2 Timothy 2:15 say concerning wisdom for those who love God?

b. (Personal) Are you willing to commit yourself to study God's Word in order to absorb His wisdom and incorporate it as part of your Christian love? What method have you found most successful for studying the Bible?

6 a. Paul goes on in Philippians 1:10-14 to list the end results of having Christ's love, wisdom and knowledge in your everyday life. List as many things as you can find in these verses that pertain to this understanding that God will give to the Christian.

b. (Personal) Have you ever experienced any of these insights from God (see Phil. 1:10-14) or had opportunities to share your faith because of trouble? Has someone else's life encouraged you as you have seen God work out problems in his or her life? Share if possible, without using any names.

THIRD DAY: Read Philippians 1:15-19.

1. What motives does Paul state that other Christians have for preaching Christ while Paul is in prison?

2. According to Philippians 1:18, how does Paul feel about all who preach the Lord Jesus Christ?

3. What similar thing did the Lord Jesus say to His disciples in Luke 9:49,50?

4. What happened in the Old Testament when Moses was told about two prophets? What did Joshua tell Moses to do about these prophets and what was Moses' reply? (see Num. 11:24-29).

5. (Personal) Should there be a spirit of division and competition among true believers in the Lord Jesus Christ? Have you ever been jealous because you felt someone was being used of Christ in such a way you would like to be used? Have you ever asked Christ to forgive you for this jealous attitude? Why not stop right now and ask for His forgiveness.

6 a. **Challenge:** The following verses point out that the chief message a Christian should share is the forgiveness and love of Jesus Christ. Summarize what these verses say and relate the thoughts to your own life if you wish to.

Acts 20:28

2 Timothy 1:9-11

1 Peter 5:2,3

b. (Personal) Which of the verses above 6 was your favorite? Why? Which verse do you want to apply to your life? Ask God by the power of His Holy Spirit to supply the wisdom and energy you need for this.

FOURTH DAY: Read Philippians 1:20-26.

1. After reading this portion of Scripture, do you believe Paul was afraid of death? Give verses for your answer.

2. Why did Paul believe that it was necessary for him to live a little longer on earth?

3. (Personal) Prayerfully write out in your own words Philippians 1:20,21. If you wish to affirm that you have similar emotions to Paul's, insert your name in these verses.

4. One who has faith in the Lord Jesus Christ never needs to fear death. The following verses give assurance of this joy in death that we can look forward to as Christians.

   Psalm 31:5

   Revelation 14:13

5. What do the following verses say about death?

   Ecclesiastes 3:2

   Ecclesiastes 5:15

6 a. **Challenge:** How does Ephesians 2:8,9 speak of a similar thought to that expressed in Ecclesiastes 5:15?

   b. (Personal) As you look back over these verses, which concern life and death, which one was a new thought, personal challenge or a real encouragement to you?

21

FIFTH DAY: Read Philippians 1:27-30.

1. What challenge does Paul give these beloved Christians in Philippians 1:27?

2. We are to lead consistent lives as Christians. The following verses speak of this matter. What warnings and challenges do you find for yourself in these verses?

    2 Timothy 3:7

    James 3:13

    2 Peter 3:10,11,13

3. (Personal) Which of these verses presented the greatest warning or challenge to you? Be specific! Share with your group if possible.

4. **Challenge:** Second Peter 3 speaks of the second coming of Jesus Christ our Lord. Read all of 2 Peter 3 and write down the most challenging or newest thoughts you find in this chapter.

5. How does Paul warn the Philippians Christians about their enemies? (see Phil. 1:28-30).

    6 a. We do not have to fear. What promise do you find about this in Isaiah 41:10?

b. Which verse did you choose to memorize this week? Write it down here.

SIXTH DAY: Read all the Notes and look up the Scriptures.

1. What new thought did you find helpful in the Notes?

2. What personal application did you select to apply to your own life this week?

Study Notes

The apostle Paul, inspired by the Holy Spirit, wrote this letter to the Philippian church while a prisoner in Rome. In it he portrayed Jesus Christ as our joy and hope. Writing to the very first church founded in Europe, Paul was called to Philippi through a vision, "Come over to Macedonia and help us" (Acts 16:9, *NASB*). Paul and his companions crossed the Aegean Sea from Troas to Neapolis, and walked some 8 to 10 miles up and over the coastal range to the city of Philippi.

God had called Paul to preach the gospel in a very strategic area. First of all Philippi—named after Philip of Macedon, the father of Alexander the Great—was famous for its gold mines. These mines had been worked as far back as the time of the Phoenicians. There had also been silver mines here and, therefore, Philippi had become a great commercial center of the ancient world.

Philippi was also known as the gateway to Europe, as its site was on the chain of hills that divided Europe from Asia from the east to the west. The hills dipped into a pass where Philip situated the city. The road between Europe and Asia wound through this pass in the mountains.

Philippi was known as a miniature Rome. Rome was proud of this colony and even made it exempt from taxation. The city planners determined to make Philippi as similar as possible in design and architecture as Rome itself. Since Philippi was a miniature, the Roman language was spoken, Roman dress and customs were observed, Roman titles used for city leaders, and, of course, Roman government ruled the city. A glimpse of Roman pride can be found as they make the charges against Paul and Silas, "These men are Jews, and are throwing our city into an uproar by advocating customs unlawful for us Romans to accept or practice" (Acts 16:20,21, *NIV*).

Yet with all this Roman influence, God used Paul to preach the gospel, and Philippi became the birthplace of European Christianity. There was the conversion of Lydia, the slave girl, and the jailer (see Acts 16). This all happened on Paul's second missionary journey about the year A.D. 52 when Paul first came to Philippi.

Paul certainly had happy memories from Philippi, which were partially responsible for his ability to rejoice in jail as he wrote this letter. He could look back to the day when Lydia and all of her household responded and believed his message concerning the Lord Jesus Christ (see Acts 16:12-15). He probably remembered with great joy how the slave girl was delivered from a "spirit of divination" through the power of Jesus Christ's name. As a result of her deliverance from this demonism there was a jailer who was ordered to physically beat Paul (see Acts 16:23).

After Paul was beaten, he and Silas were cast into a slimy, dark prison and chained to the wall. As Paul wrote this letter, he undoubtedly remembered the great earthquake that God brought about to loose their chains and open the doors to the prison to release Paul and Silas. The greatest joy in this memory was the fact that the jailer and his whole family believed in the Lord Jesus Christ on that very night because of this great happening (see Acts 16:27-34).

As Paul sat in prison thinking about his days in Philippi, he must have pondered how God had worked during pleasant times and ugly times in the prison cell. He must have thought of the placid days of prayer and teaching while he stayed in Lydia's household as an honored guest and teacher. He probably thought of the pain and fear that he and Silas experienced when the Romans charged them before the magistrates and sentenced them to the terrible beating (see Acts 16:20-22). Yet as Paul thought about all of these things he could rejoice. He realized that God had done a work through all of these activities and formed a strong, faithful and joyous group of believers in the Lord Jesus Christ because of his preaching the first time in Philippi.

When you find yourself in a hard place, in fear, pain or terror, just remember how God used Paul's experience! You may feel chained to an office desk or kitchen sink, but be like Paul and remember what God has been doing in your life, instead of becoming discouraged over your present situation. As you praise God for what He has done in the past, you will be reminded of what He has promised to do for you always! "Rejoicing in hope, persevering in tribulation, devoted to prayer" (Rom. 12:12, *NASB*; see also John 14:1; 2 Cor. 12:9; 1 Pet. 4:12; 5:6,7).

Are You Willing to Be a Servant? Philippians 1:1,2

As was the custom, Paul started his letters by introducing who the letter was from and then greeting its recipients. Paul referred to himself and Timothy as bond-servants of Christ Jesus. In some versions the translation is slaves of Jesus Christ. By making the statement he declared his absolute dedication to the Lord Jesus Christ. He was declaring what 1 Corinthians 6:20 says: "For God has bought you with a great price. So use every part of your body to give glory back to God, because he owns it" (*TLB*).

Yes, God had bought Paul with the price of His own Son, the Lord Jesus Christ. Paul presented his life in absolute obedience to Christ through this statement. In Acts 20:28 he said, "Feed the church of God, which he [the Lord Jesus Christ] hath purchased with his own blood" (*KJV*). To be Jesus Christ's slave is the way to perfect freedom!

Perhaps you have feared to call yourself a servant of Jesus Christ because it might mean that your freedom would be exchanged for an unhappy experience of bondage. Perhaps you have thought the Lord Jesus would call you to work for a cause for which you were not suited! God who has made you will never do such a thing. He has a plan for your life, and is only waiting for you to submit your will to this plan so that He can work it out to His glory, which in turn will bring you great happiness.

Often we are like a split personality, willing to give half of ourselves to God and yet wanting to reserve the other half for our own use and desire. This never works! The letter to the Romans explains why. "Do not let sin control your puny body any longer; do not give in to its sinful desires. Do not let any part of your bodies become tools of wickedness, to be used for sinning; but give yourselves completely to God—every part of you—for you are back from death and you want to be tools in the hands of God, to be used for his good purposes . . . . Thank God that though you once chose to be slaves of sin, now you have obeyed with all your heart the teaching to which God has committed you" (Rom. 6:12,13,17, *TLB*).

> *Paul had joy because he gave himself totally to God.*

Perhaps the following story will illustrate how the Christian who tries to keep one foot in the world and one in the Lord's plan is really not very useful to the Lord at all. Chuck Boreski, a geologist, decided to enter a centennial beard-growing contest. His distinctive outfit was actually three separate changes of clothing, skillfully folded to give him the impression of two sides of a geologist—one vintage 1875 and the other, 1975. He said, "On one side I dressed like a prospector, because that's how field geologists looked in 1875. On the other side I wore a business suit, because that's how oil geologists look today." He also had his hair and beard trimmed to fit the style of each side of his costume. His comment was, "I think that's what cost me the contest."

Today there are Christians who wonder why they are "losing the contest" of serving God to the fullest. Could this be your situation? Paul had joy because he gave himself totally to God. If he could talk to you today he would say, "I urge you therefore, brethren, by the mercies of God, to present your bodies a living and holy sacrifice, acceptable to God, which is your spiritual service of worship. And do not be conformed to this world, but be transformed by the renewing of your mind, that you may prove what the will of God is, that which is good and acceptable and perfect" (Rom. 12;1,2, *NASB*). Are you willing to pray and ask God to prove His will in your life as you present your body a living sacrifice to Him? Only then will you find that His ways will really satisfy you, as they are acceptable and perfect.

Set Apart Because of Our Faith

Paul addressed his letter to "all the saints in Christ Jesus." The term *saint* in our day sometimes paints a picture of an unworldly pious person. However, in the Hebrew usage the basic idea is that this person is different from others, set apart in a special way because of his or her faith in Jesus Christ. Paul called these people "saints in Christ Jesus." In all of Paul's letters he often used these phrases: *in Christ*, *in Christ Jesus* and *in the Lord*.

In Christ Jesus occurs 48 times in all of Paul's letters. When Paul used this phrase he clearly meant that a person in Christ Jesus was truly a Christian believer, a saint set apart for His use. He meant that these people were living continually conscious of the Holy Spirit of Christ within them, conscious of God speaking to them in the world moment by moment, and conscious that they were never separated from the presence of the Lord (see John 14:16,17; Heb. 13:5). As a Christian are you always conscious of the encircling presence of the Lord Jesus Christ? Are you always conscious that the Holy Spirit, the Comforter, abides within you forever? You are never alone if you are "in Christ Jesus" by faith in Him.

Paul's greeting to his friends was "grace, and peace," which comes "from God our Father, and from the Lord Jesus Christ." Grace—*charis*—was the normal Greek greeting, and peace—*eirene*—was the Hebrew greeting. Each of these words was made more precious by the new meaning given to them by Christ. The word *grace* gives the basic idea of joy, pleasure, brightness and beauty. The Christian has become a child of the love of God by his faith in Jesus Christ. Grace is often defined as *G*od's *R*iches *A*t *C*hrist's *E*xpense.

The word *peace* never simply means the absence of trouble. It suggests total well-being, harmony, an undisturbed state of mind, absence of mental conflict and a serenity because we are "in Christ Jesus."

So when Paul prayed for grace and peace for the Philippian Christians, he was praying that they would have the joy of knowing God as the Father and the peace of being reconciled to God through the grace of Jesus Christ. This is the great privilege and joy every Christian experiences when he or she comes "in Christ Jesus" to God. "For God is not *the author* of confusion, but of peace" (1 Cor. 14:33, *KJV*). Have you received the grace and peace of the Lord Jesus Christ? (see also Eph. 2:8,9; 1 Cor. 1:4; 1 Tim. 1:14).

Be Thankful for Those Special People Philippians 1:3-11

Happy memories of the Philippian Christians were part of the reason for Paul's ability to rejoice in jail: "I thank my God upon every remembrance of you" (Phil. 1:3, *KJV*). Paul had built a close and loving relationship with these Philippian Christians so that he could say, "I have you in my heart" (Phil. 1:7, *KJV*). Their relationship was so beautiful that he could say, "Only God knows how deep is my love and longing for you—with the tenderness of Jesus Christ" (Phil. 1:8, *TLB*). Paul was expressing here how much he loved these people and how his heart ached for a reunion with them.

What about you? Do you have similar emotions about special Christians God has sent into your life? Are you thankful for these people who have loved you "in Christ Jesus"? If so, why not stop right now and write a letter, give them a call or make a special visit to express your thanksgiving and to renew your fellowship with these Christians who have blessed your life and encouraged your Christian growth?

Paul lived to pray for others. So it should be for every true Christian friend, father, mother, brother or sister. Do you have a prayer list? Do you talk to the Lord about your friends? Do you rejoice in prayer for answers from God? (See Ps. 116:2; Eph. 1:16; Phil. 1:6; 2 Tim 1:3.) Are you challenged to pray this prayer? "We will give ourselves continually to prayer, and to the ministry of the word" (Acts 6:4, *KJV*).

Paul prayed that the Philippian Christians' love would grow more and more in real knowledge and discernment. He wanted them to have the power to judge rightly and follow the right course of action. He also wanted them to have a familiarity, awareness and understanding of God's plan for their lives.

God wants you as a Christian to grow more and more in His wisdom and knowledge. The Lord Jesus said that it was necessary that He go away so that the Holy Spirit could come and give us wisdom and knowledge (see John 16:7-14). The Holy Spirit will guide you into all truth and help you to understand spiritual matters as you read the

Bible and seek His leading. Of course your foundation must be faith in the Lord Jesus Christ before you can be led by the Holy Spirit into the wisdom and knowledge of God. "Other foundation can no man lay than that is laid, which is Jesus Christ" (1 Cor. 3:11, *KJV*).

It was Paul's prayer that these Christians' love would grow not only in knowledge and judgment, but also that they would have an intelligent love that would give them a right sense of values (see Phil. 1:10).

This was a vital concern to Paul for he viewed this in light of the coming day of Christ. When Christ comes, the only gift we will be able to present to Him will be ourselves. Thus Paul pointed out here not only to the Philippians, but also to use in this age, that our supreme goal should be to be "filled with the fruits of righteousness, which are by Jesus Christ" (Phil. 1:11, *KJV*). Discerning love will always result in a bumper crop of this kind of fruit!

The Importance of Prayer

Now Paul had been praying all of these things for the Philippians, being confident that Jesus Christ who began the good work in them would perfect it unto the day that they stand before Jesus Christ (see Phil. 1:4-6,9).

Prayer plays an important role not only for ourselves to grow in God's love, wisdom and knowledge, but also to rejoice and pray for others as Paul did.

There was once a nurse who taught a sick man to pray and in so doing changed his whole life. He had been despondent, but he changed to a man of real joy. Since much of the nurse's work was done with her hands, she used her hand as a prayer reminder. Each of her fingers stood for someone she wanted to pray for and she told this disgruntled man about her system of prayer. Her thumb was nearest to her and it reminded her to pray for those who were nearest and dearest to her. Since her second finger was used for pointing, the second finger in prayer stood for all her teachers and those who helped her in her spiritual life. The third finger is the longest and so it stood for all the important leaders in every sphere of life whom God has instructed us to pray for (see 1 Tim. 2:1-5). Since the fourth finger is the weakest finger of the hand, she used this finger to help her to remember to pray for those who are weak, in pain and in trouble. The nurse's little finger was her smallest and most important, and so she chose this finger to remind her to pray for herself. Perhaps you might like to try this system of intercessory prayer, as you're driving, or walking about your home, or anytime you have a free moment to be with the Lord.

To the Praise and Glory of God

Before we leave this section and as we think of the fruit of righteousness spoken of in Philippians 1:11, let us remember that it is to be used to "the glory and praise of God." There are some Christians who would like to put on the appearance of being so faultless that they make other people turn away from Jesus Christ. There are some Christians who are hard, harsh and judgmental because they think they are so pure. There are some Christians who are so critical that they actually repel others from being interested in the love of Jesus Christ. Paul is praying that all Christians will have the kind of love and gentleness that will attract others to Christ.

Be an Ambassador Wherever You Are Philippians 1:12-15

Paul wrote to the distressed Philippians and told them that what might have appeared to them as a setback really was an important advancement for Christianity. For not only had the entire praetorian guard learned of Christ because of this, but also the local Christians had been encouraged by Paul and were openly and fearlessly sharing the truth of Jesus Christ.

Paul spoke of himself as "an ambassador in bonds" (see Eph. 6:20). The short length of chain that bound his wrist to the wrist of the soldier who was his guard was actually the link in the chain that helped him to witness for Christ! There would, of course, be a round of guards assigned to this duty both night and day. All of these guards knew why Paul was imprisoned—because of his faith—and many of them were touched by the message of Jesus Christ and became real believers. "My imprisonment in the cause of Christ has become well known throughout the whole praetorian guard and to everyone else" (Phil. 1:13, *NASB*).

> *God is able to give you the courage*
> *and joy to speak the Word of God*
> *without fear just as He gave courage*
> *to Paul and his fellow Christians.*

You may consider yourself in prison in your office, home, neighborhood or city. But remember that God wants you to use your opportunity just as Paul did! God is able to give you the courage and joy to speak the Word of God without fear just as He gave courage to

Paul and his fellow Christians in their day (see Phil. 1:14). Paul set the example first by concentrating on happy memories of how God had blessed his life and the lives of others, and then engaged in prayer asking God's blessings on all of those he knew and met. If you follow his formula, you will have a great impact in the place where God has put you, whether it be a prison or a palace.

As Long as God's Kingdom Is Advanced Philippians 1:16-18

While Paul was gone other men preached Jesus. Some had pure motives while others had selfish ambitions and used this opportunity to advance their own influence and prestige. Paul showed no personal resentment toward them, however, and said that as long as Jesus Christ was preached he would rejoice (see Phil. 1:18). The Lord Jesus Christ had set this same example (see Luke 9:49,50).

What about party spirit within our churches today? There should never be a spirit of division and competition among true believers in the Lord Jesus Christ. Have you ever felt jealousy in your heart because you felt someone was being used for Christ in an outstanding way and that you were left on the side lines? Actually you should rejoice that anyone is being used effectively, if they are preaching Jesus Christ. We need to recognize that God gives everyone special abilities (see Eph. 4:11-13). Why not choose to rejoice when you see a person winning others to the Lord? Often God allows one person to sow the seed and another to harvest it! (see John 4:37).

There Will Be a Happy Ending! Philippians 1:19-26

Paul truly believed that the present opposition he was experiencing would work out for good (see Rom. 8:28), because the Christians were praying. He expected deliverance through the provision of the Spirit of Jesus Christ, perhaps not from prison, but, in any case, deliverance from being put to shame in anything concerning his Christian testimony (see Phil. 1:20). Paul's chief goal in life was to bring glory to Christ, whether he lived or died (see Phil. 1:21).

We can sense how much Paul loved the Lord by his statement, "Sometimes I want to live and at other times I don't, for I long to go and be with Christ. How much happier for me than being here!" (Phil. 1:23, *TLB*). Yet Paul was willing to stay on earth because he could be "of more help to you by staying!" (Phil. 1:24, *TLB*). Paul was anxious to see the Philippian Christians progress in their joy in the faith, and this was why he wanted to live and come to them again to teach them more (see Phil. 1:25,26: 2 Cor. 4:5; 1 Pet. 5:2,3).

How much do you care about the spiritual growth and joy in the faith of others? There are shepherding needs in every church and Bible study group for those who are willing to teach the Word of God or perform other services for the Lord (see Acts 20:28; 2 Tim. 1:9-11). Are you willing to be open to what God has planned for you to bring joy and faith to others and to encourage fellow Christians as they progress in their faith? Will you bow your head right now and simply tell God that you are willing to be His instrument, available for whatever service He may call you?

God's Challenge to You Philippians 1:27-30

Paul made it plain to the Philippians living in a Roman colony that they needed to stand fast in their faith and realize the responsibility of their citizenship in the kingdom of God. He also expected them to have a unity because of their common faith in Jesus Christ (see Phil. 1:27). We need to remember that all true Christians are bound together in one Spirit even today.

When Christians stand fast because of God's strength, it causes nonbelievers to realize that Christians have something that they do not possess. In today's world of turmoil, people seek for self-preservation and want to share in the calm courage reflected in the Christian life (see 2 Cor. 4:8-10).

UNITED IN LOVE
PHILIPPIANS 2

Before you begin each day:
1. Pray and ask God to speak to you through His Holy Spirit each day.
2. Use only your Bible for your answers.
3. Write your answers and the verses you have used.
4. Challenge questions are for those who have the time and wish to do them.
5. Personal questions are to be shared with your study group only if you wish to share.
6. As you study look for a verse to memorize this week. Write it down, carry it with you, tack it to your bulletin board, tape it to the dashboard of your car. Make a real effort to learn the verse and its reference.

FIRST DAY: Read all of Philippians 2 concentrating on verses 1-4.

1. How did Paul ask the Philippian Christians to "complete my joy" in Philippians 2:2?

2. What attitudes and actions must Christians receive from Christ in order to complete Paul's joy? (see v. 1).

3 a. (Personal) Do you believe there are qualities God wants to give you to bring joy into others' lives? Reread Philippians 2:1. Be honest in your analysis of your life, and make a list of your strengths and weaknesses. Will you pray and ask the Lord Jesus to help you to complete joy in someone's life this week as you let the Holy Spirit work in and through your own life?

b. Read Philippians 1:11. Share with your study group or with another Christian what this verse means to you.

4 a. Paul knew whether he was free or a prisoner that God would supply strength, joy and hope daily through the fellowship of the Spirit of God. What do the following verses say about the provision God makes for every Christian through the third person of the Trinity, the Holy Spirit?

Romans 15:13

2 Corinthians 13:14 (This was Paul's farewell message to the Corinthians.)

1 John 4:13

b. Which of the verses in 4a was a new, challenging or encouraging thought? Share with your study group, if possible.

5. **Challenge:** Look at Philippians 2:3 and try to explain in your own words what this verse means, or write down the verse from a Bible version that has been most helpful to you.

6. How is the last half of Philippians 2:3 completed by the words in Philippians 2:4? Try to give illustrations of how these thoughts could be carried out if a Christian willingly allows the Holy Spirit to control his life in the areas that Philippians 2:3,4 covers.

SECOND DAY: Read Philippians 2:5-11.

1. Whose "mind" or "attitude" is the Christian to allow to empower and purify his or her thoughts and actions?

2. How does Philippians 2:5-8 describe how the Lord Jesus Christ humbled Himself?

3 a. (Personal) Reread if possible Philippians 2:5-8 in several different Bible versions. Have you ever thanked the Lord Jesus Christ for the things He has done for you? Why not pause and thank Him again if you have already realized His great love and sacrifice for you?

   b. (Personal) Does Christ's example challenge you to make any changes in your life? What are the changes you want the Holy Spirit to do inwardly and then work outwardly through your life? Make a list here. Share a few of these changes, if at all possible, to help and encourage others.

4. Because Christ willingly humbled Himself, God exalted Him (raised Him to a high level). How does Philippians 2:9-11 describe Christ's exaltation, "raised to the highest position?"

5. **Challenge:** We know that today there are many who do not bow their knee to Jesus and call Him Lord of all. When is the time when all people shall finally have to admit and confess this, and bow to the Lord Jesus? Read the following verses and use your own words to put down the key thoughts.

   Acts 10:36,42

Romans 14:10-12

2 Peter 3:7-10

6. The Scriptures state it is God's desire that all people would be saved, but always indicate that not all will choose to be saved from their sins. The Lord has made a provision through the death and resurrection of His only Son for forgiveness of sin and the gift of eternal life. Sadly, some people may never accept this loving gift offered to them by the heavenly Father. Read John 3:3, 16-18 and Hebrews 9:22. Then write out your thoughts concerning God's love and forgiveness.

THIRD DAY: Read Philippians 2:12-18.

1. Philippians 2:12 may puzzle you. Personal salvation— forgiveness and cleansing—is given by God through faith, apart from any human works. How does Ephesians 2:7-10 clearly explain this truth?

2. (Personal) What have you been depending on to get you to heaven? If God were to ask you why He should let you into heaven, what would your reply be after reading Ephesians 2:7-10?

3. According to the Philippians passage, who plans the good works for each Christian and provides the power for these good, godly works to be accomplished through a mere human creature? Please give the verse.

4 a. **Challenge:** God provides the inner source of power for the Christian in the third Person of the Trinity, the Holy Spirit. How does the Holy Spirit strengthen and guide the Christian? As you read each of the following verses, insert your own name into these verses if you wish to claim these promises from God.

Romans 5:5

Romans 8:26

1 Corinthians 2:13

Hebrews 9:14

b. Which of the verses in 4a helped you to appreciate the power of the Holy Spirit in the life of a Christian? Explain your answer.

5. Name the qualities that should be a sign of Christ's dwelling in a believer's life, according to Philippians 2:14-18.

6 a. What did Paul say about himself in Philippians 2:16,17?

b. (Personal) Do you believe God could give you this same motive and desire for another person's faith in Christ and spiritual development? Are you willing to pray and ask God to give you the same burning heart for another's spiritual welfare?

FOURTH DAY: Read Philippians 2:19-30.

1. What did Paul always want to hear and know about people who had believed in Christ?

2. (Personal) If someone has believed in Christ because of your life and words, do you just leave them alone or do you share Paul's attitudes?

3. What kind of follow-up love, interest and concern do you believe Christians should be willing to do in our present society to encourage those who are new in their faith in Jesus Christ?

4. What kind of follow-up was Paul planning for the Philippian Christians, according to this passage?

5. How does Paul instruct the Philippian Christians to receive Epaphroditus?

6. (Personal) After reading Paul's instructions on how the Philippians should receive Epaphroditus, what thoughts do you have concerning your church missionaries, pastors, teachers and other workers? Are you as gracious, thoughtful and helpful toward them while they are at home as when they are abroad? How could you improve this situation?

FIFTH DAY: Read 1 John 4:1-21 with 1 John 5:1-4.

Paul was full of love for the Philippian Christians. Read these passages in 1 John and choose at least five verses that are helpful to you, ones you might like to share with other people. You may choose to pray that God will work on some of these areas in your life this year.

Share some verses with your group if possible.

1.

2.

3.

4.

5.

6. Which verse did you choose to memorize this week? Did you rejoice over its promise from God?

SIXTH DAY: Read all the Notes and look up the Scriptures.

1. What new thought did you find helpful in the Notes?

2. What personal application did you select to apply to your own life this week?

Study Notes

The Holy Spirit gives us in the apostle Paul a wonderful example of a Christian life. Paul urged that we follow in the steps of Jesus Christ, taking the path of servanthood. In Philippians chapter 2 we are urged to complete our Christian lives by living together in love and unity. "Look not only to your own interests, but also to the interests of others. Your attitude should be the same as that of Christ Jesus" (Phil. 2:4,5, *NIV*). What this verse instructs the Christian to do is not easy. It means to love without compromise! (see also 1 John 3,4,5).

Dwight L. Moody said, "Strife is knocking others down; vainglory is setting oneself up." In Philippians 2 we are instructed to think of others as better than ourselves. In other words we need to be willing to say, "The Lord Jesus Christ is first, others are second, and I am willing to be third."

Who can give an ordinary human being the strength to choose this kind of love? "I can do all things through Christ which strengtheneth me" (Phil. 4:13, *KJV*). This can be the only answer to the source of joy and strength that comes from the Lord alone! The word *joy* occurs in this short letter to the Philippians 16 times.

Paul could be called the "rejoicing apostle." Perhaps you'd like to read the whole letter at one sitting and underline the words: *joy, rejoice, be glad, Jesus Christ* and *Lord*. Through Paul's words we are commanded to rejoice, and if we refuse to rejoice, we will know only discord. Joy helps when you are suffering trials. Others will be attracted to the Lord Jesus Christ if you are a joyful Christian! You, too, will have joy in the midst of trials if you are willing to rejoice in the Lord!

It hardly seemed possible that Paul was writing from prison with chains holding him, for his writing revealed he had a light heart and it was evident that his soul was free! There was no atmosphere of depression and disillusionment in his confinement, but only a reflection of the joy of the Lord. Paul mentioned the Lord Jesus Christ's name 40 times in this short letter.

Some of the most wonderful things concerning the Lord Jesus Christ and the Christian life are found in Philippians. It tells you how your life may be purified, dangers avoided, and progress made if you are willing to trust Jesus Christ by making Him your joyful Savior and Lord (see 2 Tim. 1:1,9,10; Heb. 7:25; 2 Pet. 1:3,11).

Look First to the Interest of Others Philippians 2:1-4

Paul was proud of these Christians in Philippi. Their dedication had thrilled him and he wanted them to keep growing in their faith in the Lord Jesus. Notice that the first verse begins with the condition *if.* Paul used this term many times to mean "in view of the fact that there is encouragement from being united with Christ." What is the comfort Paul referred to? There is the comfort of the Lord Jesus Christ's love and forgiveness (see Rom. 3:24-26); there is His tenderness and mercy for you (see Luke 4:18,19; John 10:10); and there is the constant fellowship of the Holy Spirit (see John 14:16,17,26).

In view of the fact that Paul and the Philippians had Christian love for one another, he challenged them in this letter to be united in their love and convictions and have a common purpose and mind. Paul stated that this was the one thing that would make him completely happy (see Phil. 2:2). To be of accord and mind does not mean that you have to be a duplicate of every other Christian! God doesn't expect us to Xerox copies of each other or "yes" people! It does mean that we need to seek a common ground of agreement, although we may disagree on minor points of doctrine. The Philippians had harmony of thought concerning salvation in the Lord Jesus Christ, and eternal life and joy found in Him (see John 3:16-18).

Paul saw this unity achieved as every Christian offering his or her life as a sacrifice to the Lord (see Rom. 12:1). There was one danger Paul felt that could threaten the joy of the Philippian church, and that was disunity. This is the danger that threatens the fellowship of Christians today. "Do nothing from selfishness or conceit, but in humility count others as better than yourselves. Let each of you look not only to his own interests, but also to the interests of others" (Phil. 2:3,4, *RSV*).

Here Paul stated the three great reasons for discord in the church both in that day and today. First, there is selfish ambition where people work to advance themselves rather than the cause of Christ. Second, there is the desire for personal prestige, which is often a greater temptation than wealth. It is a natural desire to want your opinion sought, and to be known by name and appearance as an authority in the church. Yet this is the extreme opposite of what a spiritual person of God should desire.

When a Christian does good deeds, they should be done to glorify the Father who is in heaven rather than to glorify the self. Such good deeds should focus men's eyes upon God. Third, there is the desire to have your own interests fulfilled. This is the kind of person who wants to conquer others and always wins the argument! This person considers everyone else an opponent who must be pushed out of the way to clear the path for his own victory. If a person concentrates on his own self-interests, there can be no unity!

Paul gave the solution to power struggle. First of all if we have faith in Jesus Christ this gives us unity with one another. Then the power of Christ's love will keep unity, as we humble ourselves before one another and think of the other person as better than ourselves. This does not mean that we will love only those who love us, but that we must by Christ's strength love even those who hate us!

Christ can give us the power to love people we don't even like.

Christ can give us the power to love people we don't even like. The Holy Spirit that's shared by Christians will shed abroad the love of God within your heart and enable you to live a life of love (see Rom. 5:5). Even Aristotle said, "Men were never meant to be snarling wolves, but to live in fellowship together." Yet humility is not a human virtue. Political candidates do not point out the virtue of their opponents or vice versa! Humility is the precious root God plants in the heart of the Christian. It's up to you to be willing to be humble, to feed upon God's Word and spend time in prayer, in order that humility may sprout and go deep into your life. If we allow the Lord Jesus Christ to increase in our lives, we can solve many of the problems in personal, neighborhood and church relationships!

The story is told of two young artists who both hoped to obtain success, yet they were so poor they could not go to school to study art. The pair decided to draw lots to see which one would study while the other worked to support them. Then when the artist who had been in school made enough money from the sale of paintings to support them, the other would stop working and go to art school.

Dürer was the one to have the first opportunity to study, while Knigstein began working at hard labor. Dürer sold several pictures and now it was the other man's turn to study. Sadly, however, Knigstein found that his fingers had become so stiff and gnarled from heavy labor that he could never work with an artist's brush. Therefore, he sadly resigned himself to give up all of his artistic dreams, yet was not embittered by the experience. Shortly after his discovery, Dürer found him kneeling by his bed with his hands uplifted in prayer. The artist heard his friend unselfishly praying for the continued success of his friend, since he himself could never be an artist. Dürer hurriedly sketched the expressive hands of his friend and later completed the now famous painting known as "The Praying Hands." This painting has brought comfort and courage to countless millions around the world.

How much of self do you sacrifice for others? If you want joy and victory in your Christian life, then put Jesus first and ask Him to plant the root of humbleness within your own life. Allow it to grow as you daily read the Bible and fellowship with the Lord in prayer. Will you choose to allow Christ to encourage and empower you to put another's welfare ahead of your own interests?

Delight Yourself in the Lord

Psalm 37:4 says, "Delight thyself also in the Lord; and he shall give thee the desires of thine heart" (*KJV*). There are many things in which we can delight. For some, delight is food, drink, talk, sports, music, literature, drama and art. Some are engrossed in the stock market and their spirits rise or fall with the market's ups and downs. Humans all seek to delight themselves in something, but God, the Creator of our universe who made us, knows our innermost longings and desires. We can never delight ourselves in the psalmist David's God until we crown Him as Savior and Lord. "But as many as received him, to them gave he power to become the sons of God" (John 1:12, *KJV*).

With the promise in Psalm 37:4, as in any contract, there are conditions to be fulfilled. Sometimes we are prone to skip our part, all the while expecting God to do His part! Delighting ourselves in the Lord in a practical way means doing what Paul told the Philippians to do in Philippians 2:2-4. Thus we will be going God's way, honoring Him and worshiping Him. We will find our life's ambitions will be pleasing to God and will bring unity with fellow Christians. This is why Paul said, "Make my joy complete by being of the same mind" (Phil. 2:2, *NASB*). We will be happier, more effective persons as we follow Paul's advice and delight ourselves in the Lord.

Christ Provides Our Model Philippians 2:5-11

The language of Philippians 2:5-11 is poetic. Paul set down a hymn that may have been used in the early church's worship, or it could have been composed as Paul was led by the Spirit in writing this letter. This hymn speaks of Christ's humiliation and exaltation.

The passage teaches the deity of Christ for He was in the "form of God," the second Person of the Godhead, absolute God, "equal" with God (see John 1:1,2,14; 10:30; Phil. 2:6,11; Col. 1:17). This hymn is intended to give Christ the honor due Him, and is similar to the one sung in Revelation: "Thou art worthy, O Lord, to receive glory and honour and power: for thou hast created all things, and for thy pleasure they are and were created" (Rev. 4:11, *KJV*). Similar thoughts speaking of the Lamb of God (see John 1:29) are given in the hymn: "Worthy is the Lamb, the Lamb that was slain, to receive all power and wealth, wisdom and might, honor and glory and praise" (see Rev. 5:12).

Although Christ was the Son of God, He humbled Himself and left His heavenly home to come to earth as the God-Man—taking the form of a man. He became the Author of life to those who would believe by becoming obedient unto death—"even the death of the cross" (see Phil. 2:8).

The Lord Jesus did not leave heaven reluctantly but "for the joy that was set before him" he endured the cross (Heb. 12:2, *KJV*). He humbled Himself and came to earth with joy.

There were seven steps in His humbling described by Paul in this hymn. The first step was when He left heaven's glory. The second step was when He made Himself of no reputation (see Phil. 2:7). He came down to this earth a helpless baby, yet within Him existed the power to speak this universe out of existence! He was God (see Col. 2:9). He placed upon Himself limitations as He laid aside His heavenly glory. He did not lay aside His deity but He did allow Himself to get weary, to sit down at a well, and finally to be crucified. When we turn to His final prayer recorded in John 17:5, we can see what this means: "And now, O Father, glorify thou me with thine own self with the glory which I had with thee before the world was" (*KJV*).

The third step in the humiliation of Christ was His taking upon Himself the form of a servant (see Phil. 2:7). God's Son was in a poor peasant family. The fourth step was that He allowed Himself to be "made in the likeness of men." He came in the human line, born of a virgin, and took upon Himself human flesh. This was truly humiliation—the human mind cannot even comprehend.

The fifth step in our Lord's humiliation is found in Philippians 2:8: "And being found in fashion as a man, he humbled himself" (*KJV*). For instance, when the soldiers came to the Garden of Gethsemane to arrest Jesus Christ, He went forward to meet them and asked, "Whom seek ye?" They said, "Jesus of Nazareth." He answered, "I am he." Then for a moment His glory shone forth and they fell back. Yet Christ humbled Himself and allowed them to arrest Him in that garden as a common criminal (see John 18:1-13).

The sixth step in Christ's humiliation was when He "became obedient unto death" (Phil. 2:8, *KJV*). "No man taketh it from me, but I lay it down myself. I have power to lay it down, and I have power to take it again" (John 10:18, *KJV*).

The seventh and last step in Christ's humiliation was His obedience to death upon the cross (see Phil. 2:8). The public execution in Old Testament days among Jews was done by stoning, not by hanging. Death by crucifixion was the Roman method. Under the Mosaic system when a Jewish criminal committed a terrible crime he was executed by stoning and then his body would be strung up on a tree for the public to view. "Christ hath redeemed us from the curse of the law, being made a curse for us; for it is written, Cursed is every one that hangeth on a tree" (Gal. 3:13, *KJV*). Christ left heaven's glory and came down to this earth to the cross to pay the penalty for our sins. He is the holy, righteous God who came to earth in order to show love and mercy to you. Have you ever received Him into your life? (see Rev. 3:20).

Christ was exalted and given a name above every name. In Philippians 2:10,11 we read "That at the name of Jesus every knee should bow, of things in heaven, and things in earth, and things under the earth; and that every tongue should confess that Jesus Christ is Lord, to the glory of God the Father" (*KJV*). This means that even those who are doomed to hell because of their unbelief in the Lord Jesus Christ will have to bow to Him because He is Lord. Those who turn their backs on Him on earth will have to finally acknowledge the Lordship of Christ.

Today each individual has the freedom to choose whether or not to bow down to Christ and call Him Savior and Lord, but the day will come when even those who rejected Him will have to acknowledge that He is Lord of all (see 1 Cor. 15:28; Rev. 5:13). The fact remains that there are still many people today who still reject the Lord Jesus Christ, but as the Scriptures show, one day they will have to acknowledge that He truly is the Lord of lords, who visited this earth that those who would receive and believe in Him might have everlasting life. "Jesus saith unto him, I am the way, the truth, and the life: no man cometh unto the Father, but by me. If ye had known me, ye should have known my Father also: and from henceforth ye know him, and have seen him" (John 14:6,7, *KJV*; see also Acts 4:12; 1 Pet. 1:3,18,19; Heb. 5:9). "And this is the record, that God hath given to us eternal life, and this life is in his Son. He that hath the Son hath life; and he that hath not the Son of God hath not life: (1 John 5:11,12, *KJV*).

Christianity—A Life and a Creed Philippians 2:12-18

Paul was a practical man. He always showed Christians a way to act out their faith. Christianity is both life and a creed. If a person has only a creed without a life to match it, it amounts to very little. After Paul takes us to the heights of Christ's exaltation, he has no intent of leaving us there. He said, "Dearest friends, when I was there with you, you were always so careful to follow my instructions. And now that I am away you must be even more careful to do the good things that result from being saved, obeying God with deep reverence, shrinking back from all that might displease him. For God is at work within you, helping you want to obey him, and then helping you do what he wants" (Phil. 2:12,13, *TLB*).

In the *King James Version* it reads, "Work out your own salvation." Work out means live out, not working for eternal life, but showing the work that God has planned for your life as you yield yourself to His power daily. This is an absolutely personal matter that no one can do for you. If you have invited Christ into your life and God has planted in your heart salvation in Christ, then you are to live out the salvation. You can go about it with confidence as you rely on the Holy Spirit's power. "For it is God which worketh in you both to will and to do of his good pleasure" (Phil. 2:13, *KJV*).

Since Christ lives in the Christian in the person of the Holy Spirit, you have an inner source of direction and power for God's plan for your life! Are you willing to yield yourself to His plan and power each day? What do you think He has planned for your life today? Are you willing to give Him first priority in your life?

You may be thinking about overwhelming problems in your own life right now and wondering if Christ is sufficient. You need not fear or tremble! Let God put your overwhelming problems into perspective. God does not want you to worship your problems nor to ignore them, but He wants to come in to be your strength and help. Someone has said, "God has no problems . . . only plans." Since God permitted the problems to come into your life, He wants to use them to help you have a deeper knowledge of Himself and His love for you. "Moreover we know that to those who love God, who are called to his plan, everything that happens fits into a pattern for good. For God, in his foreknowledge chose them to bear the family likeness of his Son" (Rom. 8:28,29, *Phillips*; see also Rom. 8:31-39).

Your Attitude Is Showing

"Do all things without murmurings and disputings" (Phil. 2:14, *KJV*). If we are going to "glow" for God, we can't be grouchy and grumpy! (see Matt. 5:16). If you have committed your life to the control of the Lord, you are under His orders. Don't complain, "If God is my Lord, why did He allow this thing to happen to me?" No one asks his Commander-in-chief the "why" of anything He asks you to do. Obey

Him and then you will shine in the world like "bright stars" and be genuine children of God!

> *If you feel you have come to the end of yourself, remember that this is when God can begin to work!*

Yes, there may be times when we fail to have the right attitude when trouble comes along. We may even fall flat in the process, but as we confess the sin of rebellion and distrust in God (see 1 John 1:8,9), we can grow in our Christian faith. Many lessons can be learned through this fire that refines, purifies and often charts a new course for your life. So if you feel you have come to the end of yourself, remember that this is when God can begin to work! Pray and commit all of your problems to Him and trust Him to work them out to make you more like Himself and to bring glory to Himself.

Will you allow the Lord to work in your life in this way? Then God can say, "Behold, I have refined thee, not with silver; I have chosen thee in the furnace of affliction. For mine own sake, even for mine own sake, will I do it" (Isa. 48:10,11, *KJV*).

When Helen Keller, blind from birth, was asked what she considered to be the greatest tragedy that could befall a person, she instinctively responded, "To have sight but lack vision." This was the spiritual sickness Paul did not want the Philippians to have! God does not want us to "catch" this illness today either! We may have our minds full of facts and compiled statistics of world conditions, rates of population growth, and cultural differences, but what God wants us to do is to incorporate all of these things into our "spiritual vision," and hold the torch of God's Word high so that others can catch sight of the Lord Jesus Christ. How is your spiritual vision?

Paul was the supreme example of a person who had "spiritual vision." Not only did he lift up the "Word of life," but he followed upon those who received Jesus Christ, even writing them letters while he was in prison to encourage their faith and to rejoice over them! Paul showed us the joy of the Christian life lived as a sacrifice to the glory of God. "Thus you will be my pride on the Day of Christ, proof that I did not run my race in vain, or work in vain. But if my life-blood is to crown that sacrifice which is the offering up of your faith, I am glad of it, and I share my gladness with you all" (Phil. 2:16,17, *NEB*).

Are you willing to pray and ask God to give you the same attitudes of love, concern and prayer for your fellow Christians that Paul had for those of his day?

Always Put Your Trust in the Lord Philippians 2:19-30

Paul hoped to come as soon as possible to the Philippian Christians and, until he did, he hoped to send Timothy with news of the court's decision on his case (see Phil. 2:19-24). In the meantime he told these people that he would send Epaphroditus who had been their own messenger to Paul in his distress. Epaphroditus had been very ill, but for a worthy cause. "He nearly died for the work of Christ, risking his life to complete your service to me" (Phil. 2:30, *RSV*). Epaphroditus was not being sent home because he was homesick, though he did long for all his fellow Christians in Philippi (see Phil. 2:26); rather he was returning there so that Paul would be less anxious about his fellow Christians in Philippi. Paul could send word with Epaphroditus concerning his situation and his joy in his circumstances, and he knew that the Philippians would also rejoice at seeing him once again.

The closing thought in this passage, which could have been the key to Paul's joy in every situation of life, is the statement that he made in Philippians 2:24: "I trust in the Lord" (*KJV*). He trusted in the Lord that he would shortly come to Philippi himself. But as we have read this whole chapter we see that Paul always put his trust in the Lord. This is the only way that Christians can relax and rejoice in their circumstances!

Rejoice in the Lord!
PHILIPPIANS 3

Before you begin each day:
1. Pray and ask God to speak to you through His Holy Spirit each day.
2. Use only your Bible for your answers.
3. Write your answers and the verses you have used.
4. Challenge questions are for those who have the time and wish to do them.
5. Personal questions are to be shared with your study group only if you wish to share.
6. As you study look for a verse to memorize this week. Write it down, carry it with you, tack it to your bulletin board, tape it to the dashboard of your car. Make a real effort to learn the verse and its reference.

FIRST DAY: Read all of Philippians 3 concentrating on verses 1-7.

1. Paul seemed to be drawing his letter to a close in repeating a message which he never grew tired of telling Christians. What did he tell these Christians to do in Philippians 3:1?

2. How can a Christian rejoice in a world so full of sorrow? Only by keeping his or her hopes, mind and eyes on Christ! What did the Lord Jesus say to His followers about His joy in John 16:22, 24?

3. (Personal) What do the verses above mean to you today?

4 a. What does Paul warn all Christians about in Philippians 3:2?

   b. What book has God given us today so that we may test what men say in their speeches and conversations and find out if it is true to what God says?

   c. How does Paul state we are to worship God, and what does he say about "the flesh" or "external ceremonies"? Give verse, please.

5 a. **Challenge:** Today many people wear certain signs such as a cross or fish to identify themselves as Christians. This is not wrong, if their heart is in fellowship with Jesus Christ and they have true faith in Him as their Savior and Lord. God wants us to have no confidence in the flesh. In other words you are not to trust in any external ceremony but to trust in the Lord Jesus Christ with all your heart. Read Deuteronomy 30:6, which describes what a person must let God "touch," "cleanse" and "change."

   b. Read Philippians 3:4-7. Was Paul circumcised as a Jewish person? What does he say in Philippians 3:7 about all of the things he discussed in these verses?

   c. (Personal) Has your heart ever had Christ's mark of love placed upon it as you have invited Him into your life as your Savior and Lord? (see Rev. 3:20). If so, think about your past and present honors. Is anything more valuable to you than Christ's forgiveness, love and constant companionship? (see John 17:25, 26).

6 a. What does Romans 1:16,17 say?

   b. **Challenge:** How does Romans 1:16,17 confirm what Paul stated in Philippians 3:4-7?

   c. (Personal) Are you "justified," or in other words "forgiven," and in God's eyes seen "just as if you'd never sinned" because of your faith in His only Son, Jesus Christ? If so, are you helping others to discover this great joy and rejoicing in the Lord?

SECOND DAY: Read Philippians 3:8,9.

1. What does Paul call Christ in this passage of Scripture?

2. What does Paul consider the most important thing in his life?

3. What has Paul lost for his faith in Christ? Does this bother him?

4. (Personal) Have you ever suffered any loss as a result of being a Christian? Do you carry resentment because of this, or do you allow God to give you Paul's attitude of joy? Be specific! Share if possible your joy to encourage others who may have to suffer loss for Christ's sake.

5 a. According to Philippians 3:9 whose righteousness does Paul depend upon and how is the righteousness (perfection in God's sight) obtained?

b. (Personal) Whose perfection would you rather depend upon, yours or God's? Why? (see Isa. 64:6).

6. (Personal) What do the following verses say concerning righteousness and how to obtain it? Put your name into these verses if you wish to do so.

Romans 6:16-18

2 Corinthians 5:17

THIRD DAY: Read Philippians 3:10,11.

1. What four things did Paul state he wanted to experience in his Christian life in Philippians 3:10?

2 a. What do you believe Paul meant when he said he wanted to "know Christ"? As you consider that Paul was a prisoner when he wrote this, how do the following verses help you to understand Paul's statement that he wants to "know Christ"? Use your own words if you wish to.

Romans 8:35-37

2 Timothy 1:12

b. How do you believe you can get to know Christ in your circumstances? How does John 8:31 indicate you can know God?

3 a. How can an ordinary Christian understand and know the power of Christ's resurrection? (see Rom. 8:11,34; Phil. 3:10).

b. (Personal) Have you ever experienced the resurrection power of Christ as expressed in 2 Corinthians 4:16? Write down the verse. Share your experience, if possible.

4 a. How is it possible to know the fellowship of Christ's sufferings? (see Rom. 8:35-39; Phil. 3:10).

b. (Personal) Have you ever experienced any of these sufferings and yet felt His conquering power and love fill your life by the empowerment of the Holy Spirit? You may want to look up Colossians 1:27.

5. **Challenge:** When Paul in Philippians 3:10 said "made conformable unto his death" the original text gave the meaning of "continually dying to self-desire" and being willing to do the will of God, as Jesus Christ always did. How does Galatians 2:20 add to Paul's words "conformable unto death"?

6 a. To know Christ as Savior and Lord is to know that you will be resurrected from the dead because of your faith in Him as your Savior and Lord. What did the Lord Jesus say concerning the Resurrection in John 11:25?

b. **Challenge:** What do the following verses say concerning the Resurrection?

Ecclesiastes 12:7

2 Corinthians 5:1

FOURTH DAY: Read Philippians 3:12-16.

1. Did Paul claim to be perfect in his Christian walk?

2. Have you ever been disgusted, discouraged or disenchanted with a Christian or a church member who has failed to follow Christ? What does Paul say that you should do in Philippians 3:13,14 in such a situation?

3. Matthew 7:3-5 gives good advice to those who constantly are looking at others' lives rather than looking to Christ and obeying Him. What does Matthew 7:3-5 say concerning this? You may put this into your own words.

4. **Challenge:** In Philippians 3:15 the word perfect in the original text means "mature in faith in Jesus Christ." What was Paul's plea to mature Christians in this verse?

5. Paul urged all Christians to obey the truth God had revealed to them. We become strong Christians as we obey the truth of God from the Bible. The following verses outline steps in spiritual

growth. In your own words, what do they say?

2 Timothy 3:16,17

● 1 Peter 2:2

6. (Personal) Which of the above verses do you feel the Lord wants to work out in your life so that you can begin maturing more each day in your Christian life?

FIFTH DAY: Read Philippians 3:17-21.

1. Paul urged other Christians in Philippians 3:17 to follow his example and to notice others who have followed the pattern he had given for a joyful Christian life. What does he say about those who do not by faith walk in Christ's path? (see Phil. 3:18,19).

2. Ephesians 5:3-6 describes the type of person Paul spoke of in Philippians 3:18,19. Read through the verses in Ephesians. What warning does Ephesians 5:7 give a Christian?

3. **Challenge:** Read Ephesians 5:8-11 and summarize it in your own words or write it from your Bible.

4. Since it is obvious that we need a strength outside ourselves to follow Paul's example of the Christian life, what is the source of strength Paul had and God promises to give every Christian? (see Rom. 8:11 and 2 Tim. 1:7,14).

5 a. **Challenge:** What exciting statements did Paul make in Philippians 3:20, 21?

6. Which verse did you choose to hide away in your memory this week? Write it here with its reference—book, chapter and verse.

SIXTH DAY: Read all the Notes and look up the Scriptures.

1. What new thought did you find helpful this week?

2. What personal application did you select to apply to your own life this week?

Study Notes

Paul wrote to his beloved Philippians that Christ is the true and genuine source of joy. By the power of the Holy Spirit, he wrote it for Christians today. He stated that it is the privilege of every Christian to be joyful, "Finally, my brothers, rejoice in the Lord" (Phil. 3:1, *NIV*). Every Christian is to be joyful, for a long-faced Christian is the worst advertisement for Christianity! The world doesn't want a greater burden; it wants a lighter heart. Yet, how can a Christian be joyful in a world so full of sorrow? Paul gave us his answer while he was a prisoner; he said, "Rejoice in the Lord."

True Goals vs. False Goals Philippians 3:1-7

God has blessed the church. In 200 years there were already millions of Christians in the Roman Empire. No other group has ever grown and flourished in spite of great persecution as has the church of Jesus Christ. No wonder Paul began this chapter by saying, "Rejoice in the Lord." The Apostle had tremendous hope for all who had faith in the Lord Jesus Christ!

There are no accidents in God's dealings; all things have a divine purpose; the church flourished under tremendous persecution and grew stronger. Many times God allows difficulties and unexpected calamities to overtake us, but never without using them for a good purpose. You need to receive these troubles with a faith that looks beyond the present rather than rebelliously questioning why God allowed such things to happen in your life. Eternity will reveal the sufficient and wise purpose for all that happens to you. "In the same way, we can see and understand only a little about God now, as if we were peering at his reflection in a poor mirror; but someday, we are going to see him in his completeness, face to face" (1 Cor. 13:12, *TLB*).

Alexander Duff was a missionary who sailed for India on a ship called the *Lady Holland*. Duff had everything he owned on board the ship including his clothes, his prize possessions and his library of 800 books. When they were within a few miles of India's coast the ship met with disaster and sank. All the passengers were saved, but all their belongings were lost.

When Alexander Duff reached shore he looked back, hoping that some part of his luggage might be floating up on the beach. Suddenly he saw something very small floating on a wave. It came nearer and nearer as he anxiously watched from shore. Finally he waded into the water and found his packaged Bible! He took this to be a sign of the Lord's blessing on his mission to India.

The very next day he began his first meeting with a group of five boys under a banyan tree, reading from the Bible he had rescued from the waves. Within a week the class had grown to 300 listeners! Several years later a beautiful chapel stood on the spot where the banyan tree had been and 1000 students of the Bible raised their voices in prayer and praise to Jesus Christ! Alexander Duff's shipwreck had "fallen out rather unto the furtherance of the gospel" (Phil. 1:12, KJV).

> By waters still, or troubled sea,
> Still 'tis God's hand that leadeth me!
> —Gilmore

Back to the Basics

Yes, Saul of Tarsus was a man of rich religious background, seeking the very best, and he went from one religion to Christianity. He was an earnest searcher of truth, and blameless as far as the Jewish law was concerned (see Phil. 3:6), but he found nothing that satisfied him. One day Christ found him, and a great change came about in his life. He gladly sacrificed everything and counted the treasures of this world as nothing in comparison with Christ. He set a new standard of values and a new reason for life (see Rom. 1:16,17; 1 Cor. 1:21-25; Gal. 4:4,5; Rev. 3:20). Have you ever had this important experience? If so, how are you sharing the Lord Jesus Christ with others?

In Philippians 3:1 we read, "It doesn't bore me to repeat a piece of advice like this, and you will find it a safeguard to your souls" (*Phillips*). Paul stated what we might call a necessity of repetition. He planned to write down the warnings he felt were necessary for these Christians, which perhaps he gave them verbally when he was with them. Now like any good teacher, he was not afraid to repeat them as a reminder of their importance.

We expect to eat bread and to drink water every day for life. Also, as Christians we need to listen again and again to the truth, which is the Bread of Life (see Matt. 4:4; John 6:41,50; 1 Cor. 11:26), and the Water of Life (see John 4:13,14; 7:38,39; Rev. 21:6,7). No Christian should find it difficult or uninteresting to go over and over the great basic truths of the Christian faith. We may like fancy things at our meals, but the basic foods are essential and necessary for good physical health. So it is with the preaching and teaching of side issues, which may be attractive and have their place, but it is essential that the fundamental truths of the Bible be continually taught along with them.

"Beware of dogs, beware of evil workers, beware of the concision" (Phil. 3:2, *KJV*). What did Paul mean by this statement? Dogs here means "evil men" (see Ps. 22:16; Isa. 56:10,11). In the original writings Paul used the word *katatome* or *concision* rather than the word *peritome*, which means "circumcision." Thus, concision means those who have cut the flesh as forbidden by the Mosaic law (see Lev. 21:5). Paul put this word in to describe a forbidden self-mutilation such as castration. "For it isn't the cutting of our bodies that makes us children of God; it is worshiping him with our spirits. That is the only true 'circumcision.' We Christians glory in what Christ Jesus has done for us and realize that we are helpless to save ourselves" (Phil. 3:3, *TLB*).

According to Jewish beliefs, circumcision was ordained by God as a sign and symbol that they were the people with whom God had entered into a special covenant relationship (see Gen. 17:9,10). But with Christ's coming, circumcision is only a sign in the flesh. If a man is to be near to God something far more is needed than a mark on his body (see Deut. 10:16). "For the Lord seeth not as man seeth; for man looketh on the outward appearance, but the Lord looketh on the heart" (1 Sam. 16:7, *KJV*).

Paul described the change in evaluating things after Christ found him (see Phil. 3:4-7). He stated that of all men he could have taken confidence in his flesh, having been circumcised on the eighth day as was the Jewish custom (see Gen. 17:10-13). He pointed out that he was a Hebrew, a word which was supposed to be connected with the name of Eber, who was an ancestor of Abraham (see Gen. 10:24; 11:14-26; 14:13). He declared himself to be a Pharisee, which was a sect of Jews who studied much and had many traditions in regard to fasting, washing of hands, the Sabbath, etc.

The Pharisees were the most influential group of Judaism at the time of Christ and the strictest sect (see Acts 26:5). They were a fraternal order that formalized the religion of the scribes by placing it into practice. That is why the scribes and Pharisees are often mentioned together in the New Testament, for the scribes were the learned men who made the systematic study of the law and its exposition, their professional occupation. In Philippians 3:6 Paul mentioned his great zeal in persecuting the church and how blameless he was in following the law of the scribes.

Yet after mentioning all these things, he counted none of them as treasures and nothing in comparison to Christ! (see Phil. 3:7). As for his sincerity as a Jew he stated that he was not lacking (see Phil. 3:6)! He erased "gain" (credit) and wrote "loss" (debit). He had a new reason for life and a new standard of values. This was his choice in life! He had chosen the Lord Jesus Christ as his Savior and Lord.

John Wycliffe, who lived in the fifteenth century, had a burning desire to give to the people the Bible in their own language. In his day, Bibles were written only in Latin. The people could not read, particularly Latin, so they did not have the Word of God. Wycliffe gave his life to translate the Bible into the language of the people. When it was completed, it was so popular that the people would pay a load of hay for the privilege of reading the Bible one hour! The church leaders hated Wycliffe, and after he died he was called a heretic. He was called anti-Christ and anti-God. Nevertheless, his work was done in the Spirit and lives on for us today.

> Only one life to live
> Twill soon be past
> Only what's done through Christ
> Will last!
> —Author unknown

Have One Goal in Life Philippians 3:7-9

"But all these things that I once thought very worthwhile—now I've thrown them all away so that I can put my trust and hope in Christ alone. Yes, everything else is worthless when compared with the priceless gain of knowing Christ Jesus my Lord. I have put aside all else, counting it worth less than nothing, in order that I can have Christ, and become one with him, no longer counting on being saved by being good enough or by obeying God's laws, but by trusting Christ to save me; for God's way of making us right with himself depends on faith—counting on Christ alone" (Phil. 3:7-9, *TLB*).

Paul weighed both the world and Christ and knew the truth of the words of the Lord Jesus, "For what is a man profited, if he shall gain the whole world, and lose his own soul?" (Matt. 16:26, *KJV*). Paul was truly united to Christ. To be in Christ is to be linked to Him in a living relationship of faith so that His life pulsates throughout our beings and His power motivates and stirs us on (see John 15; Acts 17:28).

Paul called Jesus Christ "My Lord" (see Phil. 3:8). He was surrounded by people in the colony of Rome where a mere man, Caesar, was called "lord." Paul said, "Christ Jesus is my Lord. He's the one whom I worship." He goes on to say that everything is "dung." He did not trust in anything or anyone other than Jesus Christ. The One whom he once hated above all else, Jesus Christ, he now trusted above all else!

Philippians 3:9 is the verse that came to John Bunyan, as he walked through the corn fields one night. He said, "I did not see myself as only a sinner, but as sin from the crown of my head to the sole of my feet. I knew that John Bunyan could not stand in the presence of God." Then this verse came to him, "and be found in him, not having a righteousness of my own based on law, but that which is through faith in Christ, the righteousness from God that depends on faith" (Phil. 3:9, *RSV*).

What happened to the apostle Paul and John Bunyan has happened to millions of men and women throughout all ages. It is the revolution of the soul that completely changes from a faith in their own righteousness and any law they may be trying to keep to a complete faith in Jesus Christ.

Experience the Power of His Resurrection Philippians 3:10-14

"All I want is to know Christ and to experience the power of his resurrection; to share in his suffering and to become like him in his death" (see Phil. 3:10). In this statement Paul discounted all personal achievement, that he might be found "in Christ." Paul wanted to possess the experience of Christ in his own Christian life. We find him making statements such as, "That I may know Him" (see Phil. 3:10). "And be found in Him" (see Phil. 3:9). To be found in Christ means that we are blameless and complete. "That I may know . . . the power of his resurrection" (see Phil. 3:10).

The sweetest Christians we meet are those who are suffering or have some great handicap to overcome.

The power of the risen Christ is that which gives us victory over sin and death. This resurrection is the resurrection of believers into a powerful and faithful life as Christ Himself promised to give to those who would be obedient to Him. "If Christ be in you, the body is dead because of sin; but the Spirit is life because of righteousness. But if the Spirit of him who raised up Jesus from the dead dwell in you, he that raised up Christ from the dead shall also quicken your mortal bodies by his Spirit that dwelleth in you" (Rom. 8:10,11, *KJV*). "God hath both raised up the Lord, and will also raise up us by his own power" (1 Cor. 6:14, *KJV*). Paul was saying, "Now that I've come to Christ, he has become the object of my affections. I live for him and I am longing for the day that I'll come into his presence. In fact, I am willing to suffer for him by the power of the resurrection which he has put within me." Paul said, "that I may know . . . . the fellowship of his sufferings" (see Phil. 3:10).

Paul knew that there was no other way of being drawn closer to Christ except through suffering. The sweetest Christians we meet are those who are suffering or have some great handicap to overcome. The following is a portion of a letter from a woman who is in real trouble. "I asked you to pray for healing for me. Within one year I lost my mother under tragic circumstances; my husband went broke and we lost our home; and I was found to have cancer which necessitated the removal of both breasts—all this while trying to raise three wonderful children. Truly God's grace is sufficient, but I need prayer for courage. But, oh, what I am learning in the furnace!" This woman went on to write about how she had been drawn closer to Christ through these experiences.

>"Crown Him the Lord of life,
>Who triumphed o'er the grave,
>And rose victorious in the strife
>For those He came to save;
>His glories now we sing
>Who died, and rose on high,
>Who died eternal life to bring,
>And lives that death may die!"
>—Matthew Bridges (1800-1894)
>Godfrey Thring (1823-1903)

Paul spoke of the "home stretch" in Philippians 3:12-14: "Not that I have become perfect yet: I have not yet won, but I am still running, trying to capture the prize for which Christ Jesus captured me" (v.12, JB). Paul was not trying to tell the Philippians he had gained absolute and final knowledge of Christ as he outlined in his letter. Rather, he was stating that the Christian needs to diligently and constantly pursue these things and have them as an ultimate goal for their lives.

Every Christian is marked! His associates watch his life to see if it measures up to that mark. Christians should be different! This means that Christians should make their decisions after first asking, "Is this God's will for me?" rather than, "Will this promote my personal welfare or make things more comfortable for me?" Being expendable for Christ is not usually glamorous at the time and often personal recognition and honor is denied that person.

"I press towards the goal to win the prize which is God's call to the life above, in Christ Jesus" (Phil. 3:13, *NEB*). Paul assured us that he did not think he had already won the prize but he chose to forget the past and strain ahead for what was to come! (see Phil. 3:13). Holding this kind of position may mean taking a stand on issues in business or professional life that could cost a promotion or salary increase. It may even cost a job. Christians who have such convictions are needed in legislative groups where they will have the courage to vote against legislation that is not good for the country. They will not be popular with pressure groups, yet that stand may sometimes buy the time needed for wiser decisions to be made!

> *Once you have committed yourself to the Lord Jesus Christ He will sweep you up in the thrill and excitement of reaching full maturity.*

The Christian should deny himself choices in life that may be all right in their place, but will interfere with his or her reaching the prize (see Phil. 3:14). Once you have committed yourself to the Lord Jesus Christ He will sweep you up in the thrill and excitement of reaching full maturity and nothing will keep you from wanting to witness, grow and be more like Christ.

Paul may have been particularly interested in speaking to antinomians. This was a sect who denied that there was any law in the Christian's life. They taught that if Christians were within the grace of God by faith in Jesus Christ, it didn't matter what they did; God would forgive them. They felt quite safe and taught that no further discipline or obedience to God was necessary. Paul was pointing out here that until the very last day of the Christian's life we are to live as an athlete pressing onward to a goal that is always out front. No one ever graduates from the Christian life!

If we are honest in our experience with God He will make it plain to us that we must never relax in our efforts or lower our standards, but press on to the goal He has set for us. Satan will try to lead you into situations that are revolting to you. All you need to do is trust Jesus Christ and resist the devil (see Jas. 4:7, 1 John 4:4).

If you put on Christ by cultivating His presence through Bible reading and prayer, letting Him speak to you through prayer and His word, worshiping Him, spending time with other Christians, serving Him, and turning every room in your being over to Him, then your higher nature will be nourished and you will be spiritually victorious in your own special "race."

You Are a New Creature Philippians 3:15-21

The Bible tells us that we have two natures within us. In fact, the apostle Paul told of his own experience: "The good that I would I do not: but the evil which I would not, that I do" (Rom. 7:19, *KJV*). Yet there is victory over the human nature as stated in 2 Corinthians 5:17: "If any man be in Christ, he is a new creature: old things are passed away; behold, all things are become new" (*KJV*).

When we come in faith to the Lord Jesus Christ our eyes are opened and we are given a new direction; our hearts are changed. We need to choose to let Christ be the Lord of our lives. It seems quite clear that there were some who were teaching that it was now possible to be "perfect" in a final sense. Paul's approach to this was that the truly mature Christian would know better and that God would reveal this truth to him (see Phil. 3:15). True persuasion concerning this would have to come from God through the ministry of the Holy Spirit: "He will guide you into all the truth" (John 16:13, *NASB*).

Philippians 3:16 is perhaps more difficult to understand! Vincent (*Word Studies,* p.451), interprets the verse to mean, "Whatever real Christian and moral attainment you may have made, let that serve as a rule for your further advance." *Beck* translates this verse, "Only be guided by what we have learned so far." In other words, Paul seemed to be saying that real progress will be made along the lines that they have already learned and practiced. The *New English Bible* translates it, "Only let our conduct be consistent with the level we have already reached."

Paul used himself as an example in Philippians 3:17-21. This is not the first time in which he had used himself as an example. In 1 Corinthians 11:1, he told the Christians at Corinth, "Be ye followers of me, even as I also am of Christ" (*KJV*). Christians were to imitate him as he was following Christ.

Paul pointed out an example the Christians were to avoid (see Phil. 3:18,19). They were not to live as enemies of the cross, but were to stand for everything the cross stood for. There were many who believed that Christ's death on the cross meant nothing. The Philippians were to recognize that Christ's death on the cross brought forgiveness and a new life: "Christ hath redeemed us from the curse of the law, being made a curse for us: for it is written, Cursed is every one that hangeth on a tree" (Gal. 3:13, *KJV*). Paul pointed out that those who denied Christ's sacrificial death on the cross for man's sin would have destruction as their destiny (see Phil. 3:19).

He spoke of the god of their "belly" as being their chief concern. This reference not only means gluttony, but probably the sensual indulgences and shameful lusts in which some of these people indulged.

In contrast with this kind of life, Paul pointed out that mature Christians live as a colony of heavenly citizens whose temporary home is earth (see Phil. 3:20). We are to wait patiently and expectantly for Christ's return at which time He will bring full deliverance from all sins and illnesses, and complete the process of perfection.

What a promise Paul left the Philippians and every Christian in the last verse of this chapter! God will "fashion anew" our bodies. The full nature of the change of our bodies is not detailed in the Bible but only hinted at in 1 Corinthians 15:42-44, 49, 51-54. We do know that we as Christians will no longer be subject to death and we will be released from the limitations we now know. First John 3:2 tells us, "When he shall appear, we shall be like him" (*KJV*).

Our earthly bodies are limited, and man cannot even go into outer space without a specially equipped spacesuit! Isn't it exciting to think that the Christian will have a body throughout eternity that will be like Christ's glorious body! Many people think of Christians as having wings in heaven and just being spirits drifting out into space. But the Bible definitively says that our body will be changed from a natural body and raised into a spiritual body!

In 1 Corinthians 15:23 we read that "Christ rose first; then when Christ comes back, all his people will become alive again" (*TLB*). What a tremendous and exciting event we await; we will see the supernatural power of God in action!

Do you have faith in Jesus Christ so that you will know and see and experience this "power of His resurrection"? If you know Him you will experience having your present body, which is still subject to sin, disease and death, transformed and remodeled into a "body of glory" like the resurrection body of our Lord (see Luke 24:39; 1 Cor. 15:51,52; 1 Thess. 4:13-18). Your body will be deathless, diseaseless, sinless; it will be designed for you as a citizen of a "better country," a heavenly kingdom! This change will be brought about by Christ's great power. Do you have the Lord Jesus Christ in your life? Have you invited Him in in all of His mighty power? (see Rev. 3:20).

STAND FAST IN THE KNOWLEDGE OF CHRIST

PHILIPPIANS 4

Before you begin your study this week:
1. Pray and ask God to speak to you through His Holy Spirit each day.
2. Use only your Bible for your answers.
3. Write your answers and the verses you have used.
4. Challenge questions are for those who have the time and wish to do them.
5. Personal questions are to be shared with the class only if you wish to share.
6. As you study, look for a verse to memorize this week. Write it down, carry it with you, tack it to your bulletin board, tape it to the dashboard of your car. Make a real effort to learn the verse and its reference.

FIRST DAY: Read all of Philippians 4 concentrating on verses 1-3.

1 a. How did Paul describe his affection for his Christian friends in Philippians 4:1?

  b. The Philippians to whom Paul had preached and witnessed, and led to Jesus Christ, were like a reward, a "crown" to him. How does 1 Thessalonians 2:19 add to this thought?

2. **Challenge:** The crown Jesus Christ will give to some Christians is described in other places in the Bible. Give the name of the crown and the reason the Lord Jesus will present it to certain Christians.

   2 Timothy 4:7,8

   James 1:12

   1 Peter 5:2-4

   Revelation 2:10

3. (Personal) Will you have any crowns from the Lord?

4. a. See Revelation 4:8-11. What do these 24 Christians say to the Lord in Revelation 4:11 and what do they do with their crowns?

   b. Since the elders gave their crowns to the Lord, what do you believe other Christians will do with the crowns He has given to them?

5. a. Who is it that gives a Christian the power to live rightly in order that the Lord can give crowns for resisting temptation, for faithfulness, for suffering, for "feeding" or giving people God's Word from the Scriptures? Read Ephesians 6:10.

b. **Challenge:** Read Ephesians 6:10-18 to discover the armor with which God wants to supply each Christian. List the armor.

c. (Personal) Have you put on God's armor? Do you lack any piece of the armor? Which piece is missing in your life? Why not ask the Lord Jesus for this piece of armor and defense right now? Trust Him to give it to you and go out today protected by all of God's armor.

6 a. Two women, Euodias and Syntyche had some form of disagreement. They were both in the church at Philippi. What did Paul strongly urge them to do?

b. What did Paul ask one of his fellow workers—a true yokefellow—to do in Philippians 4:3?

c. (Personal) Has God ever asked you to be a peacemaker for Him? Have you obeyed this call? God honors those who obey this call from Him (see Matt. 5:9).

SECOND DAY: Read Philippians 4:4-7.

1. What suggestions did Paul make to the Christians in Philippians 4:4-6?

2. If you act on Paul's advice in Philippians 4:4-6, what will be the result of such obedience to God? Give the verse, please.

3. **Challenge:** How do the following verses help you to understand the "moderation" or "tolerance" spoken of in Philippians 4:5? Use your own words if you wish to.

   1 Corinthians 13:4-7 (Note: *Charity* in the *King James Version* means Christian love.)

   Ephesians 4:2,3

4. Philippians 4:6 urges Christians to pray about everything. It is God's plan that this plea follows the thoughts in Philippians 4:5. Can moderation or "gentleness in Christian love" be accomplished by human efforts or through the Lord Jesus Christ's power?

5 a. (Personal) What moderation, tolerance, or gentleness do you feel you need in your life right now? Be specific. Name the situation. Have you prayed about this situation "with thanksgiving" that God will hear and answer according to your need for Jesus' sake?

   b. Share something God has done for you in answer to prayer if it is possible to do so without mentioning specific names, etc.

6 a. Who is it that keeps our hearts and minds at peace in this world of turmoil? (see Philippians 4:7).

   b. What promise do you find in 2 Timothy 1:12,13 that is similar to Philippians 4:7? Summarize it in your own words if you wish to.

THIRD DAY: Read Philippians 4:8,9.

1. List the things with which God wants the Christian to fill his mind and continually think about.

2. The very opposite type of thoughts and actions are described in Romans 1:28-31. This passage describes the person who refused to receive God's Son as Savior. How is the Christian's mind described in this passage, and what thoughts and actions are present when Christ is not in the life?

3. What does Paul urge the Philippians to do in Philippians 4:9?

4. **Challenge:** How does a mere man, even the apostle Paul, dare to suggest that his life-style and teaching should be followed in order to fulfill Philippians 4:8? Read the following verses in Romans 5 and 6 that could help you as a Christian to allow God to use your life as a model for other Christians to follow. Personalize these verses by adding your name if you wish to.

   Romans 5:5,6

   Romans 5:17

   Romans 6:4

   Romans 6:11

5 a. What does God promise Christians who allow the Holy Spirit to work out Philippians 4:4-8 in their lives? This promise is given both in Philippians 4:7 and Philippians 4:9.

b. How does Isaiah 26:3 confirm God's plan for peace?

6. (Personal) Do you have the Lord Jesus' peace in your life's circumstances? If not, reread these passages on peace and ask God to work them out in your life. By faith in Christ commit every area of your life to the God of peace. List the areas you particularly want to commit to God and receive His peace. Do you want to ask a fellow Christian to pray with you for these things as you begin to thank God for His answers ahead of time?

FOURTH DAY: Read Philippians 4:10-18.

1 a. How did Paul live according to Philippians 4:11?

b. What kind of circumstances had God allowed Paul to experience in order that he could make such a statement? (see Phil. 4:12).

2. How did Paul describe how he had suffered for Christ's sake in 1 Corinthians 4:11-14, and why did he write about these circumstances?

3. According to Hebrews 11:25, what was Paul's attitude and what should be every Christian's attitude when suffering for the sake of Christ? Personalize this verse with your name if you wish to.

4. By whose strength did Paul live through all of the rough experiences of his life? (see Phil. 4:13).

5. (Personal) What rough trial are you experiencing right now? Will you pray and ask God to keep His promise in Philippians 4:13 in your situation? Are you willing to rely on Christ's strength —not your own—to see you through the struggle?

6. In Philippians 4:14-18 we discover that the Philippian Christians had sent help to Paul in various ways in order to further his ministry of sharing Jesus Christ's message. What did Paul say these gifts were in the sight of God?

FIFTH DAY: Read Philippians 4:19-23.

1. What promise from God is given to all Christians in Philippians 4:18,19? Write this verse inserting your own name and make it God's promise to yourself today.

2. **Challenge:** The following verses speak of God's care and supply for the Christian's life. Write them in your own words if you wish to.

   Psalm 31:19

   Psalm 57:1

3. Which of the verses in question 2 was most helpful to you? If possible share why.

4. **Challenge:** What is a "saint" according to Philippians 4:21?

5. What Christians—saints—sent greetings to the Philippian Christians through Paul's letter? Give verses.

6. Which verse did you choose to memorize this week? Write it down here. Are you praying for Christians who are not allowed to have a Bible?

SIXTH DAY: Read all the Notes and look up the Scriptures.

1. What new thought did you find helpful in the Notes?

2. What personal application did you select to apply to your own life this week?

Study Notes

The opening verse of this chapter expresses the warmth of Paul's affection for his Philippian friends. "So, my brothers whom I love and long for, my joy and my crown, do stand firmly in the Lord, and remember how much I love you" (Phil. 4:1, *Phillips*). As the shadows of Paul's life closed in around him, those he had brought to Christ were his greatest joy! In fact, he had no greater joy than to hear of their spiritual health and prosperity. His emotions were the same as the apostle John concerning his "spiritual children" as the Holy Spirit led John to write in 2 John 4 and 9: "It has given me great joy to find some of your children walking in the truth, just as the Father commanded us.... Anyone who runs ahead and does not continue in the teaching of Christ does not have God; whoever continues in the teaching has both the Father and the Son" (*NIV*).

Do You Have a Spiritual Purpose? Philippians 4:1-5

Paul began this sentence in Philippians 4:1 with the word, *therefore* (*NIV*), which would indicate that the following remarks are "in view of the heavenly citizenship and privilege it involves." His challenge to "stand fast" is a basic conclusion to his remarks in Philippians 3, where Paul wrote of Christ as being the one goal in life. He urged the believers to have spiritual purpose in their lives and a unity as believers.

In the *King James Version* we note the affection that Paul literally breathed out as he used six terms of endearment in Philippians 4:1! He called his fellow Christians: my brethren, dearly beloved, longed for, my joy, my crown and my dearly beloved.

All of these words create a vivid picture of Paul's tender affection for his fellow Christians. What an example this is for Christians today! The crown—*stephanos*—was a woven wreath awarded to a winning athlete. It was also used to be placed upon the head of a guest at a banquet. This crown signified both triumph and festivity! It was as if Paul was considering himself an athlete of Christ and because of his labor, toil and efforts he considered the Philippians his crown. There is no joy in the world to compare to bringing someone else to Jesus Christ! Paul was pleased with the evidence of the sincerity of the Philippians' faith and obedience to God. At the same time he also wanted to encourage them to "stand fast in the Lord" (see Phil. 4:1).

Hold Fast to Christ's Sufficiency

The Philippians were to be steadfast in their walk with Him, close and constant until the end of their lives! To stand fast in the Lord is to stand fast in His strength and by His help rather than trusting in yourself. Christians must recognize their insufficiency and hold fast to Christ's sufficiency.

The word Paul used for stand fast—*stekete*—is the word that would be used for a soldier standing fast in the shock of battle as the enemy surges in upon him. It is only in Jesus Christ that the Christian can resist such temptations as cowardice, weakness, depression and defeat. Safety against such temptations is to be "in the Lord" always. Thus we recognize that He is always with the Christian. We recognize that His presence is around us, about us and in us, if we have faith in Jesus Christ! (see Matt. 28:18-20; John 16:7; Eph. 6:10-18).

In Greece it was the custom for a respectable woman to be seen, heard and know as little as possible! She took her meals in her apartment and never appeared alone on the street. However, Philippi was in Macedonia and here customs were different. Women had a freedom and a place in life they had in no other part of Greece. In the narrative of Acts we read of Paul's work in Macedonia. At Philippi Paul's first contact was a prayer meeting at a riverside where he spoke to women. Here Lydia responded to the good news of Jesus Christ (see Acts 16:13,14). In Thessalonica many of the leading women came in faith to Jesus Christ and the same thing happened in Berea (see Acts 17:4,12).

Apparently there were two women in the Philippian church who were prominent and who had lately begun to irritate each other! We would like to know what the story is behind the remark in Philippians 4:2, but we don't know. Apparently these women had had some kind of quarrel or disagreement! The disagreement could have been with each other or with the church at large. It is possible that these two may have had house congregations of the church at Philippi, for we know that this was the way the people worshipped in the early church. It is interesting to see that women played a leading part in the affairs of the early congregation. Paul said they "fought side by side with me in telling the good news, and with Clement and the rest of my fellow workers, whose names are in the book of life" (Phil. 4:3, *Beck*).

To help affect the reconciliation between Euodias and Syntyche Paul appealed to a genuine "yokefellow," who remains anonymous, but apparently had a gift of being a peacemaker.

This quarrel really makes us think about Christian relationships! Suppose your life were to be summed up into one sentence. What would that sentence say about your personality? Would you like to go down in history with one thing known about you—that you could not be at peace with other Christians? Or would you rather be known as a true yokefellow with other Christians and a peacemaker? What would be the one sentence verdict on your life today?

Is Your Name in the Book of Life?

Paul referred to Clement and his fellow workers whose names are in the book of life (see Phil. 4:3). The reference to the book of life is a common Old Testament symbol for God's recognition of those who belong to Him, and appears in several passages of Revelation (see Rev. 3:5; 13:8; 20:15). Some Old Testament references concerning the symbol of the book of life are in Exodus 17:14; 32:31-33; Psalm 69:27,28; Isaiah 30:8; and Daniel 12:1. "Then they that feared the Lord spake often one to another; and the Lord hearkened, and heard it, and a book of remembrance was written before him for them that feared the Lord, and that thought upon his name. And they shall be mine, saith the Lord of hosts, in that day when I make up my jewels, and I will spare them, as a man spareth his own son that serveth him" (Mal. 3:16,17, *KJV*).

> *The most important book you can ever have your name registered in is the Lord's book of life.*

Is your name written in the book of life because of your faith in God's Son, the Lord Jesus Christ? (see Luke 10:20; John 20:31; Acts 3:19; Eph. 2:8-10). Some people consider it very important to have their name registered in the local social security or Who's Who, but the most important book you can ever have your name registered in is the Lord's book of life.

Rejoice in the Lord

"Always be full of joy in the Lord; I say it again, rejoice! Let everyone see that you are unselfish and considerate in all you do. Remember that the Lord is coming soon" (Phil. 4:4,5, *TLB*). Through these words Paul gave the deeper meaning that Christians are commanded to rejoice not because of their circumstances but because their ground for rejoicing is in the Lord. "Rejoice in the Lord" is similar to Philippians 3:1, but here there is the addition of "always," which means at all times, in all places and in all circumstances.

We are to rejoice when the circumstances are most promising and when everything is wrong for we know that God is in control no matter what the situation. "Even though the fig trees are all destroyed, and there is neither blossom left nor fruit, and though the olive crops all fail, and the fields lie barren; even if the flocks die in the fields and the cattle barns are empty, yet I will rejoice in the Lord; I will be happy in the God of my salvation. The Lord God is my Strength, and he will give me the speed of a deer and bring me safely over the mountains" (Hab. 3:17-19, *TLB*).

Sometimes Christians are very poor advertisements for the Lord. A pastor told of his congregation who recently appeared on a television program. One of the members who viewed the telecast said that if she had not been a Christian the array of solemn faces that she saw would have caused her to believe that faith in Jesus Christ makes everyone sad! Actually, those who were participating were very tense because of the new experience and therefore appeared particularly solemn. Yet many Christians do have gloomy attitudes, which in turn make them appear to have a mournful life and negates what the Christian faith really is and stands for. Christ gives real joy, and Christians should obey Paul's good advice to "rejoice in the Lord always."

You may object and say, "But if you only knew what I am facing!" Yes, but what about Paul? He had been imprisoned and beaten repeatedly. In addition, he had been stoned once, shipwrecked three times, and was often falsely accused by enemies (see 2 Cor. 11:23-30). Yet he didn't murmur or give up. In fact, he knew the secret of joy, and without boasting he could point to himself as an example for the believers to follow (see Phil. 4:9). Do you complain? Do you display a joyless attitude? If so, you are a poor advertisement for Jesus Christ.

Paul then urged all Christians to let their moderation or their gracious gentleness be known to all men. In some translations these words were translated patience, softness, modesty and forbearance. The Greeks call this quality "justice and something better than justice." If this quality was exercised among Christians it would go a long way toward eliminating any disunity that might exist! When you are upset by circumstances, it is normal to find it difficult to exercise good will and graciousness toward anyone! Yet if you have the joy of the Lord you are able to handle more effectively the problems of life and will find it much easier to be gracious to others.

George Müeller was asked, "What is the secret of joy in your life? You are always a radiant Christian. What is the explanation? Are you that way all of the time?" His answer was something like this, "No, many mornings when I get up I do not have the joy of the Lord in my life. But I get my Bible, and I read it until I have the joy of the Lord in my life." George Müeller built many orphanages in Ashley Down, England. Without a personal salary, he relied only upon God to supply the money and food needed to support the hundreds of children he befriended in the name of Christ. For many years he kept a motto on his desk that said, "It matters to Him about you." Müeller claimed God's help and rejoiced always. At the end of his life he said that the Lord had never disappointed him but faithfully always supplied all of his needs. He learned to rejoice in all circumstances and God had faithfully met all of his needs (see 1 Pet. 5:7).

There Is Power in Joy

In Nehemiah's day they had a great Bible reading. After they had finished building the walls of Jerusalem they set a pulpit at the Water Gate and Ezra read from the Scriptures from morning until midday. Many of the people had been in Babylon during the captivity and had never heard the Word of God read. At first it so overwhelmed them that they began to weep, so Nehemiah sent out a word to all of them, "Go your way, eat the fat, and drink the sweet, and send portions unto them for whom nothing is prepared: for this day is holy unto our Lord: neither be ye sorry; for the joy of the Lord is your strength" (Neh. 8:10, *KJV*). Yes, he told the people what is true today also—there is power in your joy!

Christian Joy Is Rooted in God

Happiness and joy are two different emotions. Happiness is apt to be more related to circumstances and to involve a need of gladness. Christian joy is more a delight of the mind coming from the assurance of a present or future that is rooted in God regardless of circumstances. Joy unrelated to circumstances is a fruit of the Spirit (see Gal. 5:22). It is not something that can be worked up by your own strength! The story is told of a man who had many trials and yet he was always a joyous person. One day a fellow Christian asked him, "Were you always like this?" His reply was, "No, not until I became a Christian. I used to drink heavily just because I felt so sorrowful and because I didn't want to face life. It's been wonderful to be a child of God and to have the joy of the Lord in my life!"

Paul closed his exhortation to rejoice with the words "the Lord is near," which was a watchword of the early church. These words could be another link between prayer and the expectation of Christ's early return. Some people believe that this is the meaning of this phrase. Yet it could also be an echo of Psalm 145:18; "The Lord is near to all who call upon Him" (*NASB*).

Another view of "the Lord is at hand" is that the Lord's return will come and we will all have to give an account of our lives to Him. Such a reminder should encourage us to do His will. A similar thought appears in James 5:8, "You also be patient. Establish your hearts, for the coming of the Lord is at hand" (*RSV*). Matthew Henry, the great English Bible scholar, said, "The consideration of our Master's approach and our final account should keep us from smiting our fellow servants and support us under present sufferings." This blessed hope of Christ's coming again casts its gracious influence over all of life. Paul prayed that the Christian would have joy at all times and not be worried by the cares of this world (see Matt. 24:3; Mark 13:1-37; Luke 12:40; 17:22-37; 21:5-35.)

Be Prayerful about Everything Philippians 4:6-9

Dwight L. Moody said of Philippians 4:6: "Be careful for nothing; be prayerful for everything; be thankful for anything!" Yes, the way to be anxious about nothing is to be prayerful about everything. The prayer of faith must be a prayer of thanksgiving because faith knows how much it owes to God. Put your prayers into God's hands and go off and leave them there. Do not worry about them. Give them completely to God, as the farmer gives the wheat to the soil after the soil has been properly plowed. If you do, then the peace of God will stand guard over your heart and mind (see Phil. 4:7). This is a peace that God fills the believer with as he stands firmly in position "in Christ."

Paul stressed that we can pray about everything. There is nothing too great for God's power; and nothing too small for His Father to care.

As a child can take anything great or small to a parent, so we can take anything to our heavenly Father. Just as a child never doubts that his parents will be ready and willing to listen to him, we should never doubt that God will do above and beyond what any human parents would consider doing for their child.

We can pray for ourselves, for forgiveness for the past, for the things we need in the present, and for help and guidance in the future. We can pray for others and Paul emphasizes that as we pray thanksgiving must be the universal accompaniment of prayer. We are to give thanks in laughter and in tears, in sorrows and in joys alike. By these actions we show gratitude and perfect submission to the will of God. When we believe that God is working all things together for good because we love Him, then we can really pray in this manner (see Rom. 8:28,29). It is comforting to know that the Lord who guides us sees tomorrow more clearly than we see yesterday!

Give Your Worries to God

The fruit of believing prayer will be the peace of God. This is an inward peace as you totally commit all to God. This peace "passes all understanding" and those who come in contact with a Christian are mystified by such a peace in difficult circumstances (see Phil. 4:7).

Worry is a major factor in the breakdown of personal health and may shorten your life! It is also a sin to brood over your troubles, for you are implying that the Lord is either unable or unwilling to meet your needs. When worry clouds your mind, why not take the tested and proven advice of the apostle Paul? Talk to the Lord, and trust Him to do what He knows is best for you. The old saying, "The devil trembles when he sees the weakest Christian on his knees" is still true.

Then after you have prayed, empty your mind of your worries and leave them with Christ. Set your thoughts upon the prescription for maintaining God's peace that Paul gave in Philippians 4:8,9: "My brothers I need only add this. If you believe in goodness and if you value the approval of God, fix your minds on whatever is true and honourable and just and pure and lovely and admirable. Put into practice what you have learned from me and what I passed on to you, both what you heard from me and what you saw in me, and the God of peace will be with you." (*Phillips*).

This is the kind of positive thinking that pleases the Lord, and He will give peace, strength, joy and victory to all who will obey Paul's inspired directions. Philippians 4:8 could be called a paragraph in mental health!

We Are to Teach by Example

In Philippians 4:9 Paul told the Christians to keep on practicing all of these Christian ethics and the morality they had learned from the Apostle himself through all of his life and teaching. There are tragically few Christians who can speak like this today. Yet it remains true that a personal example is an essential part of teaching. One who wants to teach others of Christ must demonstrate in actions the truth of what he expresses in words.

Is there someone to whom you would like to introduce Jesus Christ and teach His truths? If this is your desire you must know the Scriptures and trust the Holy Spirit to give you loving attitudes and holy desires in your life. You must be willing to allow the Holy Spirit to bring every thought into captivity to Christ, and then you will find that good deeds will automatically flow from such an attitude. Like our blessed Savior, we too will go about "doing good" (see Acts 10:38) and teaching not only with our words but also with our lives.

A college girl, who was a fine scholar, volunteered to be a counselor at a girls' camp. Despite her great abilities she was required to peel potatoes in the kitchen! One of the staff said, "It's too bad that a young woman of your education should have to peel potatoes." The girl who was a dedicated Christian replied, "Remember, I don't have to think about potatoes while I'm doing them." The application is obvious. You can keep your soul out of the dust no matter what your task, if you center your thoughts on the things mentioned in Philippians 4:8,9.

Let your mind dwell on Christ and He will beautify your life and allow you to radiate His love to others!

Allow the Holy Spirit to discipline your mind by dismissing suspicion and replacing it with hope and trust. Forego grudges and envy. Be appreciative, kind and gentle. Rejoice in the Lord a little more! Take pleasure in beauty and virtue. Let your mind dwell on Christ and He will beautify your life and allow you to radiate His love to others!

Learn to Be Content Philippians 4:10-23

The apostle Paul wrote his letter to the Philippians from behind prison bars, but he was perfectly content with his lot, for he had found his satisfaction in God. Despite his circumstances, his deep inner peace and assurance of the Lord's presence was unshaken. To Paul, God was the God of peace. In fact, this was his favorite title for God (see Rom. 16:20; 1 Cor. 14:33; 1 Thess. 5:23).

As the letter draws to an end, Paul expresses his gratitude for the gift the Philippians had sent to him. He knew that he had always been on their hearts and minds, but apparently the circumstances had given them no opportunity up until now to show their thoughtfulness toward him (see Phil. 4:10,14-18).

Within his thank-you portion of the letter Paul put a parenthesis on contentment (see Phil. 4:11-13). Paul wanted the Philippians to recognize that his joy was not just the satisfaction over the relief regarding his personal needs (see v.11), but that his joy arose from his concentration on the really important things. Above all, his joy came from the closeness of his fellowship with Christ on whose strength he constantly drew (see Phil. 4:13).

Aesop in one of his fables told of a tortoise who was unhappy because he couldn't fly. As he saw a bird having a good time floating through the air, he said to himself, "Oh, if only I had wings so that I could rise up and sail about as they do, then I would be content!" Calling to an eagle, he offered him a great reward if he would only teach him to fly. The bird told him this was impossible. The tortoise was so insistent that the eagle finally said, "Well, I'll see what I can do!" Carrying the foolish one to a great height, the eagle let go when the tortoise exclaimed, "I'd like to shove off now and try my hand at flying." Despite the flapping of his short legs, the poor creature went down and down until he landed on a hard rock below and was dashed to pieces! He was not satisfied with what God had created him to be and where God had put him.

Some Christians are never satisfied; they always desire to be something other than what the Lord has made them! Many a Christian has turned away from a life of fruitful service by trying to be something for which God had not fitted them. We are to be "content with such things as ye have" (Heb. 13:5, *KJV*). Everyone lives in one of two tents: either in Con-Tent or in Discon-Tent! Which "tent" do you live in today? "I have learned, in whatsoever state I am, therewith to be content," said Paul in Philippians 4:11 (*KJV*).

Contentment is never the result of multiplying riches, increasing pleasures or gaining fame. Most people who gain such things still find themselves unsatisfied. Contentment depends on conditions on the inside! Paul did not come to this happy philosophy of life in a moment. He said, "I have learned . . . to be content." Aspiring to be what we are not, or grasping after riches that elude us is not the way to happiness. Rather we need to do our very best with God's help to accomplish our life task with the talents and opportunities He has given us. What opportunities has Christ presented to you? Have you answered His call to serve Him with the strength He has promised to give? (see Phil. 4:13).

Paul closed his letter to the Philippians by giving them and all Christians this wonderful verse, "My God shall supply all your need according to his riches in glory by Christ Jesus" (Phil. 4:19, *KJV*).

The story is told of the man who had six dozen bunches of turnips for an orphanage. As he brought his gift he hoped someone else would supply the lamb to go with them. When he arrived at the orphanage, there stood a farmer waiting with a sheep that he had fattened, killed and dressed for the orphanage! A coincidence you say? Yes, but who planned it? There was no human conspiracy! God had ordered that meal by the prompting of His Holy Spirit to these two men.

We can apply this to our Christian service. To refuse to give the lamb because we cannot give turnips, or to withhold turnips because we cannot furnish the lamb is to forget that God overrules all and directs each one's partial contribution so as to supply the total need! God is a God of detail. Give what you have, and trust the Lord to supply the rest.

PART 2
COLOSSIANS

5. The Supreme Lordship of Jesus Christ
6. Grow in His Wisdom and Knowledge
7. Christ Is All-sufficient
8. Christians and Their World

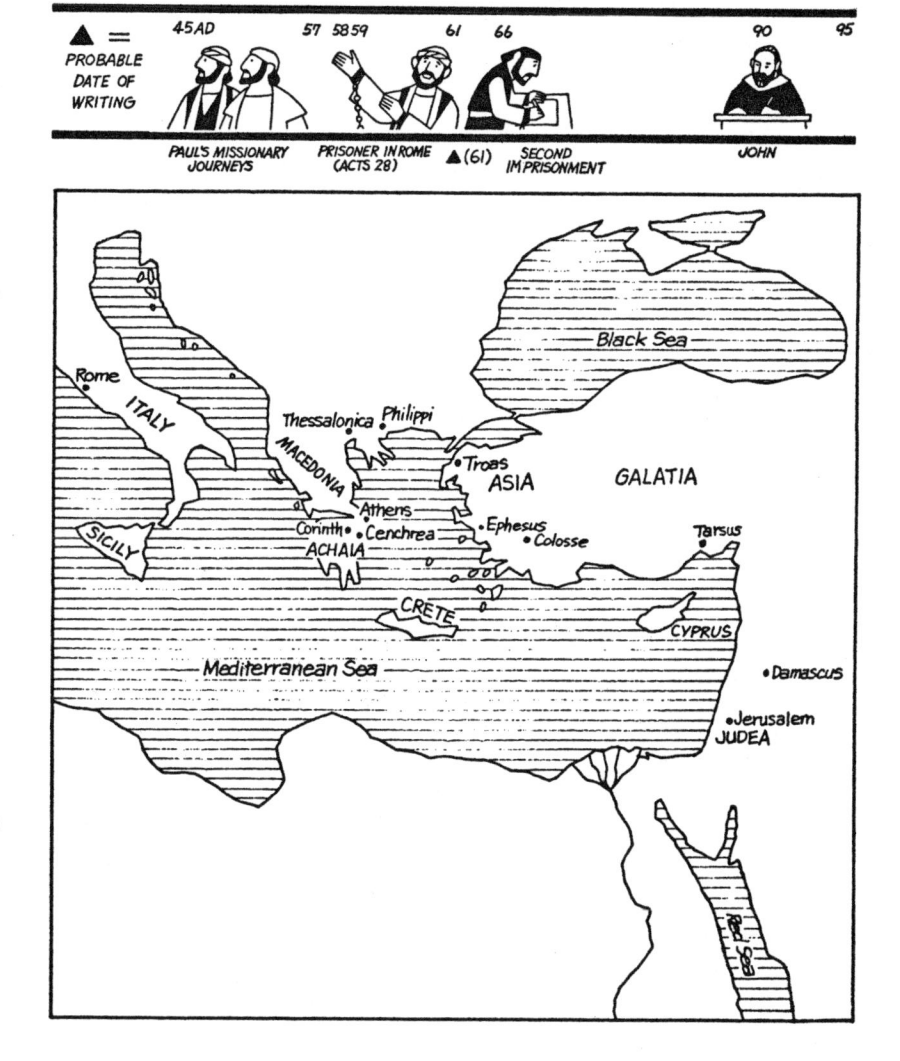

▲ = PROBABLE DATE OF WRITING

45 AD — PAUL'S MISSIONARY JOURNEYS

57 58 59 — PRISONER IN ROME (ACTS 28)

61 ▲(61)

66 — SECOND IMPRISONMENT

90 95 — JOHN

THE SUPREME LORDSHIP OF JESUS CHRIST
COLOSSIANS 1

Before you begin your study this week:
1. Pray and ask God to speak to you through His Holy Spirit each day.
2. Use only your Bible for your answers.
3. Write your answers and the verses you have used.
4. Challenge questions are for those who have the time and wish to do them.
5. Personal questions are to be shared with your study group only if you wish to share.
6. As you study, look for a verse to memorize this week. Write it down, carry it with you, tack it to your bulletin board, tape it to the dashboard of your car. Make a real effort to learn the verse and its reference.

FIRST DAY: Read all of Colossians 1 concentrating on verses 1,2.

1. According to Colossians 1, what did Paul call himself?

2. Look up the word *apostle* in your dictionary and give the definition you believe applies to Paul.

3. Timothy is also mentioned in this letter to the Colossians. What do the following verses say that would indicate why Paul considered Timothy a fellow worker and a "brother" even though there were no close family ties?

   2 Timothy 1:5

   2 Timothy 3:15

4. What does 2 Timothy 3:16, 17 say concerning the Holy Bible?

5 a. (Personal) Since the whole Bible is so important to a completely satisfying Christian life, are you willing to give God time to speak to you through His Holy Word each day? How much time will you give to God? When?

   b. How could a parent or a grandparent help their children as well as others they know to have the same privilege and heritage Timothy had?

6 a. How did Paul describe the Colossian Christians in Colossians 1:2 and what did he say was available to them from God, the Father?

   b. (Personal) What descriptive word given in Colossians 1:2 would you like to have someone use in a letter concerning you and your relationships?

SECOND DAY: Read Colossians 1:3-8.

1. What did Paul continually do for the Christians he knew? (see Col. 1:3,4).

2. (Personal) What implications does this have for the need of present-day Christians to be thankful and to pray for one another?

3 a. How does Colossians 1:4 describe the Christians in Colosse?

   b. (Personal) Would you like to be described in the same way as Paul described the Christians in Colosse?

   c. How can a Christian deserve such a fine description and reputation? Put down some key thoughts from Ephesians 2:13,14,18,19, plus other thoughts God gives you concerning faith in Christ and love for fellow Christians.

4 a. What had the Colossian Christians heard about in the word of the truth of the gospel? Give verse.

   b. Romans 5:1,2 helps us to understand the Christian's hope. What do these verses say?

5. **Challenge:** Heaven is mentioned in Colossians 1:5. Christians are promised a heavenly home when they leave their earthly residence. This is part of the Christian's hope. How do the following verses help you know about heaven?

John 14:2

2 Corinthians 5:1

Revelation 21:22-27 (Choose the highlights from this passage that are especially helpful to you.)

6. (Personal) Colossians 1:5,6 tells us that the gospel, which is the word of truth concerning Jesus Christ, brings forth "fruit." Read John 15:16,17. If you are a Christian what fruit has the Holy Spirit empowered you to bear to the glory of God? Are you like Epaphras, described in Colossians 1:7? (Note: *To minister* means "to serve.")

THIRD DAY: Read Colossians 1:9-12.

1. Make a list of the things Paul prayed for in Colossians 1:9-11. (Example: 1. To be filled with the knowledge of His will.)

2. (Personal) This is a beautiful and powerful prayer that Paul prayed for the Colossians. Would you like to have someone pray for you in this manner? Do you pray for anyone in this way? If you have a prayer notebook, why not list these requests of Paul's in Colossians 1:9-11 as guidelines for your prayers?

3. **Challenge:** Colossians 1:11 speaks of being "strengthened" by God's "glorious power." What do the following verses say concerning God's strengthening power? Personalize them with your name.

Romans 8:26

Ephesians 3:16

4. Paul prayed that Christians would know "the knowledge" of God's will for their lives. What does Romans 12:2 say about the will, or plan, God has for each Christian's life?

5. John 14:23 gives another condition for knowing and doing God's will. What does this verse say?

6. What does 2 Peter 1:3,4 say God will do for the Christian?

FOURTH DAY: Read Colossians 1:13-23.

1. How does God forgive any person's sin? Give verse.

2. Make a list of the things you learn about God's Son, Jesus Christ, in Colossians 1:15-20. Give verses. (Example: 1. The image of the invisible God—verse 15.)

3. (Personal) What new thing or wonderful reminder did you find in Colossians 1:15-20 concerning the Lord Jesus Christ?

4 a. When we receive Christ Jesus by faith how does He present us to God? Give verse.

b. What did Paul urge the Christians to do in Colossians 1:23?

6. (Personal) How do you believe Christ wants you to continue on in faith in Him? Are there any particular areas of your life where you feel you need to continue on with Christ, or perhaps begin to follow Christ in a more definite way?

FIFTH DAY: Read Colossians 1:24-29.

1. In what did Paul rejoice?

2. (Personal) Are you presently suffering for the sake of Jesus Christ?

3. **Challenge:** How do the following verses challenge you concerning any suffering brought on by faith in Christ?

    1 Peter 2:20

    1 Peter 3:14,15

    1 Peter 5:10

4 a. In Colossians 1:26 the phrase *even the mystery which hath been hid* means the Lord Jesus Christ. To whom does He want this "mystery" revealed, according to Colossians 1:27?

b. If you do not understand what *Gentile* means. look up its meaning a dictionary. Who are the Gentiles?

5 a. What was Paul's goal in life according to Colossians 1:28?

b. (Personal) Do you have a similar goal in your life? How are you asking the Lord to work this goal out through your life? What practical suggestions could you give someone who wishes to serve the Lord with these goals in mind?

6 a. Paul recognized that he could not attain his goal without the power of the Holy Spirit working in him. How does he express this thought in Colossians 1:29?

b. (Personal) Is this the power upon which you depend to accomplish God's plan for your life? (see Phil. 4:13,19, and Zech. 4:6).

c. Which verse did you choose to memorize this week? Write it here with the reference. Do you remember to pray for people around the world who have had their Bibles taken from them?

SIXTH DAY: Read all the Notes and look up the Scriptures.

1. What new thought did you find helpful this week?

2. What personal application did you select to apply to your own life this week?

Study Notes

Colossians and Ephesians were written while Paul was a prisoner in Rome. These letters contain great doctrines of the good news gospel of Jesus Christ, and were read aloud in the churches of that day. They are very similar in style, yet very different in emphasis. Ephesians talks about all believers and calls them the Body of Christ; Colossians talks about the Head of the Body—Jesus Christ. In Ephesians the church of Christ is the important theme; in Colossians the Christ of the church is emphasized. Both letters are needed, for there cannot be a Body without a Head, nor a Head without a Body.

Now, heresy had broken out in the church at Colosse, misleading the young believers. A mixture of Jewish, Greek and Oriental religions, this heresy caused them to worship angels (see Col. 2:18), and have a strict observance of Jewish ceremonies (see Col. 2:16-22). For this reason Paul felt called to make his statement of truth—the supreme Lordship of Jesus Christ—in Colossians. This letter draws a faithful portrait of Christ in all His glory and dignity, the only One to be worshiped.

Paul pointed out the failure of the Colossians to "not hold fast to the Lord" (see Col. 2:6-10,19). The place that Christ holds in any religious teaching determines whether it is true or false. Some in Paul's day, as now, thought Jesus was only a man, and Christ was the divine Spirit that came at Jesus' baptism and left Him at the cross. This meant that Christ did not die, but simply that Jesus died. You can see that this is the root error of many religions today. Modern religions based on this same old heresy misrepresent the truth in regard to Christ and His Person and work. It is good for us as we read Colossians to examine our own belief and see that we put the Head, Christ Jesus, in His rightful place in our thinking and glorify this wonderful One (see Col. 1:10-20).

First-century Colosse was an ancient but declining commercial center, about 100 miles east of Ephesus. It was situated on the Lycus Valley caravan route near the cities of Laodicea and Hierapolis (see Col. 4:13). We are not sure when the Christian message was taken there. Some believe there was an early evangelization by the Galatian Christians, while other Bible scholars believe the Colossians may have first heard the Christian message during Paul's Ephesian ministry, A.D. 53-56 (see Acts 19:10). These scholars believe the church was probably founded by Epaphras (see Col. 1:7), and consisted of Gentile Christians, including Philemon.

Paul possibly passed through Colosse on his way to Ephesus, but he was personally unacquainted with the Christians there (see Col. 2:1). Epaphras ministered to this church and was a co-worker with Paul (see Col. 1:7). We discover that he visited the apostle Paul to let him know of the progress of the Christians and also the dangerous, erroneous teaching that was misleading them. The heresy already described above was known as Gnosticism. Christian converts with an imperfect grasp of Christ may unconsciously have merged earlier beliefs with Christian concepts. Paul was very concerned with this and pointed out the error of their teaching, and in the process developed true Christian doctrine in this letter to the Colossian church. Paul sent this special letter to the Colossians by Tychicus and Onesimus (see Col. 4:7-9).

Called by the Will of God Colossians 1:1-8

Paul called himself an "apostle of Jesus Christ by the will of God" (Col. 1:1, *KJV*). An apostle was a prime minister in the kingdom of Christ, immediately called by Christ, and extraordinarily qualified. An apostle's work was to plant the Christian church and teach the Christian doctrine. Paul pointed out that he did none of this work by his own effort, strength or sufficiency, but by the free, good will of God, since it was "by the will of God" that he was called.

Paul also greeted the church from Timothy and called him "our brother." This is an instance of his humility for elsewhere he called him his son (see 2 Tim. 2:1). What an example this is for Christians who have known the Lord for many years to respect and honor the newer Christians and treat them with kindness and respect!

> *It is only in following Jesus Christ and His way that we will find true happiness, peace, joy and a true and lasting reward.*

Paul called the Christians at Colosse saints and faithful brothers in Christ. Their faith and that love depended on the hope that is laid up in heaven (see Col. 1:5). What did Paul mean by this? Was he asking the Colossians to show faith in Christ and love for their fellow Christians so that they would receive a reward in heaven some day? There was something much deeper Paul was speaking of here.

Loyalty to Christ may involve a man in all kinds of loss, pain, suffering and unpopularity. A person may have to say good-bye to many things in order to be loyal to Christ. The world who does not know Christ thinks of Christians as being foolish when they seek to serve and forgive others, and spend their lives in selfless service. The world counts on getting ahead and pushing the weaker one out of the way. They feel that the strongest and the fittest will survive. Yet God's way of love always has the last word! It is only in following Jesus Christ and His way that we will find true happiness, peace, joy and a true and lasting reward.

As we look at the word *hope,* Christ Himself may be meant here (see Col. 1:5,27). This hope is the foundation for life here on earth and also is the hope for the actual future in all eternity. If our hope in Christ is good for this life only, and no more, then we deserve more pity than anyone else in all the world (see 1 Cor. 15:19). If our hope resides in heaven, where the new age is brought about in the person of Christ, then we can have the happiness of heaven as our hope as well as the happiness of knowing Christ's presence within us on earth! What is laid out for believers in this world by Jesus Christ is much; but what is laid up for them in heaven is much more! "Awaiting our blessed hope, the appearing of the glory of our great God and Savior Jesus Christ" (Titus 2:13, *RSV*). This hope was proclaimed in Colossians, "in the word of the truth of the gospel" (Col. 1:5, *KJV*), which the Colossians had heard before the heretical teaching surfaced.

Today the word *hope* implies uncertainty. People say, I hope so. Used in this way it refers to a feeling inside a person, but biblical hope has nothing to do with feelings, for it is not found inside a person, but is "laid up for you in heaven" (Col. 1:5, *KJV*). If a person expects an inheritance from his earthly father when he is 21, he might call this his hope. It is really his right now, but he won't receive it until he's 21. Biblical hope is like that. It is the privilege of eternal fellowship with God and every believer has this hope. Do you have this hope? Are you sharing this hope with others? "But these are written, that ye might believe that Jesus is the Christ, the Son of God; and that believing ye might have life through his name" (John 20:31, *KJV*).

In Colossians 1:7 we find the only verse where Paul designated a co-worker as a "fellowservant" of Christ. This also may be indicative that Epaphras was in a sense a "fellow prisoner" (see Col. 4:10). He was the minister or deacon of the Colossians. It is possible that he could have traveled to Ephesus during Paul's three-year stay there and had come to know Christ at that time. After being taught by Paul, he may have returned to Colosse to establish the local churches. This could have accounted for the Colossians' warm attachment to Paul and Timothy (see Col. 1:7).

Undoubtedly Epaphras had told Paul about the errors that were threatening the Christians in Colosse as well as about their love for

Paul in the Spirit (see Col. 1:8). Paul was glad for the good report of these peoples' sincere love for Christ and for all Christians that had been brought about in them by the Spirit (see Rom. 5:5; 14:17). The Colossians were living in the age of the Holy Spirit who had come after Christ had ascended into heaven (see John 14:16,17; Rom. 15:13).

We Need the Knowledge of His Will Colossians 1:9-14

It is very precious to read this prayer of the apostle Paul for his friends in Christ. That is what this entire passage is about. We learn more about prayer in this passage than from almost any other part of the New Testament. First, Paul praised God for their love for him. Then he prayed that they would be able to know God's plan for their lives and then take God's power and perform His will for their lives.

Our prayer should begin with praise, and then we need to ask to be filled with an evergrowing knowledge of the will of God for us. Christians should be conscious that they are not so much trying to make God listen to them as they are trying to listen to God! We should not try to persuade God in what to do, but rather be intent on finding out what He wants us to do. Often we appear to pray, Thy will be changed, when we ought to say, Thy will be done.

Knowing God's will involves being conscious moment by moment of His presence, and listening to His guidance through prayer and the Scriptures. Prayer and action according to God's will go hand in hand. After meditation, if there is a peace in the heart and circumstances seem to fit in with what God has said, we can go out to meet life, no matter what the situation may be, by God's power as we walk in His plan! If we truly seek this knowledge, God will give "the knowledge of His will in all wisdom and spiritual understanding" (Col. 1:9, *KJV*).

Why did Paul ask that the Colossians be filled with the knowledge of His will? The Colossians were plagued with false teachers, and members of the church were being victimized by those claiming a super knowledge of divine things. They taught that this knowledge was available only through secret rites and practices, supposedly beyond the reach of the average Christian. This was why Paul used the special word for advanced knowledge—*epignosis*—in asking God to give "full knowledge" to every Christian. He also asked that they be given the wisdom to apply this knowledge to their lives. Many people who claim to have biblical knowledge fail to see the connection between God's Word and their life. They fail to see how a delinquent child or a difficult co-worker can be part of God's plan to bring them to full maturity.

My Life

My life is but a weaving
    Between my Lord and me
I cannot choose the colors
    He worketh steadily.

Oft' times He weaveth sorrow
    And I in foolish pride
Forget He sees the upper
    And I, the underside.

Not till the loom is silent
    And the shuttles cease to fly
Shall God unroll the canvas
    And explain the reason why.

The dark threads are as needful
    In the weaver's skillful hand
As the threads of gold and silver
    In the pattern He has planned.

—Author Unknown

Where Is God in Your Priorities?

In Colossians 1:10 Paul summarized what he wanted the Lord to do within the hearts of these Colossian Christians! He wanted them to be transformed in their world and in their life view (see Rom. 12:1,2). A mental transformation is a prerequisite for an ethical renewal in life. Only God could do this for these Christians, as they were "strengthened with all might, according to his glorious power" (Col. 1:11, *KJV*). Paul was challenging these Christians to rearrange their priorities and let God's power do it!

    The degree in which a person shifts from living for self to living for Christ is the measure of spiritual maturity. Since God's ways are opposed to the ways of the world, this change of attitude includes a detachment from counting the things of this world as more important than God's will. When a person rearranges his priorities, he will discover that money, fame, leisure, education and preoccupation with other things of this world become less important than knowing the will of God and doing it. Though none of these things in themselves may be wrong, it is when they begin to interfere with God's will for our lives that they become very wrong.

The battles are often waged in the theatre of the heart of man. There is always the flesh lusting against the spirit (see Gal. 5:13-26). The two are contrary to each other. The Holy Spirit constantly seeks to implement God's truth in our lives, while the devil seeks to keep us from it. This is the area where doubts and fears, lusts and passions, and our own emotions can be overcome and given victory by the Holy Spirit (see 1 John 4:4,5).

God promised the power of the Holy Spirit for the Christian to live "worthy of the Lord, unto all pleasing, being fruitful in every good work, and increasing in the knowledge of God" (Col. 1:10, *KJV*). Paul prayed that these Christians would be strengthened by this mighty power to live a life of patience, longsuffering and joy.

Paul now named the name in which prayer was made. "Giving thanks to the Father, who has qualified us to share in the inheritance of the saints in light. He has delivered us from the dominion of darkness and transferred us to the kingdom of his beloved Son, in whom we have redemption, the forgiveness of sins" (Col. 1:12-14, *RSV*; see also Acts 26:18).

In the ancient world when one empire won a victory over another, it was customary to take the population of the defeated country and transfer them to another land. The Jewish people of the Northern Kingdom were taken away to Assyria and people of Jerusalem and the Southern Kingdom were taken away to Babylon. This transfer of population was a characteristic of the ancient world, so Paul said that God had transferred the Christians into His own realm and His own kingdom. Have you experienced this transfer from one kingdom to the other? You only need to ask the Lord Jesus Christ to enter your life and the transfer takes place as you trust Him for the forgiveness of sins.

All Creation Centers in Christ Colossians 1:15-17

In this section Paul used the Greek word *ikon* for image, which meant exact reproduction. If photography was known in Paul's time, he would have described the Lord Jesus as a clear picture of the Father, not in physical appearance but in His personality and character. The Lord Jesus Christ reveals God's love, mercy and graciousness. The term *firstborn* is a technical reference to Christ's rank. He is the only Son of God (see John 3:16,17) uniquely begotten (see Luke 1:28-35). This term is used to show Christ's relationship to the Father before there was any world! It was in Christ that God became visible to man (see John 1:1,14,18).

In Colossians 1:17 it is made very clear that Christ was prior to all creation. He was the Creator Himself and all things were created for Him! He is the God of creation. All creation centers in Christ and has its consummation in Him. In fact, it is through Him that all things hold together (see Heb. 1:3). Apart from Jesus Christ, atomic fission would explode the universe! He keeps it together in the form in which He created it.

Christ Is the Head of the Body Colossians 1:18,19

These verses tell us that Christ is the Head of the Body of believers. As the head directs and controls all the activities of the human body, so Christ directs and controls all the activities of the Church, His spiritual body (see 1 Cor. 12:12; Eph. 1:22). Thus Paul continued to list Jesus' credits. Angelic powers were not building the church, as the false teachers claimed.

> *Christ made peace through the blood of His cross to reconcile all who would come in faith to Him.*

The fullness of all dwells in Christ (see Col. 1:19). The word used here is *pleroma*, which means the fullness of the powers and attributes of God. Christ contains and represents all that God is.

Stand Fast in His Truth Colossians 1:20-23

Paul again attacked the error of angelic superiority being taught to the Colossians by saying that even heavenly dignitaries need Christ's cleansing. "To reconcile all things unto himself; by him, I say, whether they be things in earth or things in heaven" (Col. 1:20, *KJV*). Yes, Christ made peace through the blood of His cross to reconcile all who would come in faith to Him. In the Old Testament the blood sacrifices were applied to objects in the Tabernacle. "Further, since we have a great High Priest [Christ] set over the household of God, let us draw near with true hearts and fullest confidence, knowing that our inmost souls have been purified by the sprinkling of his blood" (Heb. 10:21-22, *Phillips*).

Paul emphasized it is obvious that Jesus Christ is supreme and alone worthy of worship. Peace comes to a person who allows Christ to enter his life, forgive his sins and reconcile him to God in loving trust (see Rom. 5:10; 2 Cor. 5:18-20). The purpose for this reconciliation to God is given in Colossians 1:22,23: "He has done this through the death on the cross of his own human body, and now as a result Christ has brought you into the very presence of God, and you are standing there before him with nothing left against you—nothing left that he could even chide you for; the only condition is that you fully believe the Truth, standing in it steadfast and firm, strong in the Lord, convinced of the Good News that Jesus died for you, and never shifting from trusting him to save you. This is the wonderful news that came to each of you and is now spreading all over the world. And I, Paul, have the joy of telling it to others" (*TLB*).

It is important that we fully believe the truth and stand in it steadfastly—never shifting from trusting Him to save! This does not mean that we will be totally faultless and sinless before God in our human state (see 1 John 1:8,9), but we are to yield ourselves as fully as possible to God's perfect will in our lives.

Remember to Pray for Others

We need to take Paul's example of giving thanks to God for faith in others and pray always for them (see Col. 1:3). It is very disheartening to hear irresponsible criticism that is purely negative in nature. Note the following words of Theodore Roosevelt, "It is not the critic who counts, not the man who points out how the strong man stumbled and fell, or where the doer of deeds could have done better. The credit belongs to the man who is actually in the arena; whose face is marred by dust and sweat and blood; who strives valiantly; who errs and comes short again and again . . . and spends himself in a worthy cause; and at the best knows that in the end the triumph of high achievement, and who, at the worst if he fails, at least fails while daring greatly." Do you pray for your Christian brethren rather than irresponsibly criticizing them with purely negative attitudes?

Step on a man's toe. Watch his face and see the pain expressed. The connection of Christ—the Head, and His body— the Church, is so close that suffering in the body registers in the Head. The world hates Christ's body as it hated Him. We need to uphold one another in prayer, encouraging each other, rather than delighting in the criticism of other members of our body.

Have You Received God's Gift? Colossians 1:24-29

Paul spoke of his suffering and rejoiced in the fact that he could suffer for Christ and His mystical Body, the Church. Paul's great contribution to the Christian faith was that he destroyed forever the idea that

God's love and mercy were the properties of any one people or nation (see Col. 1:27). Paul set out to let everyone in this world know that there was one thing available to every person and that was the Lord Jesus Christ.

Not every person can master every skill, appreciate beautiful art or music. Not every person can be a great student, writer, singer or speaker. But the one thing every person can have is faith in the Lord Jesus Christ. Jesus is a gift from God, and God wants every person to receive that gift (see John 3:16,17; Rev. 3:20). He is available to every person, and God wants to give His transforming power, which can bring holiness into the life of each man, woman and child through His only Son, Christ Jesus. "God chose to make known how great among the Gentiles are the riches of the glory of this mystery, which is Christ in you, the hope of glory" (Col. 1:27, *RSV*). This is the truth of the crucified, resurrected and ascended Christ lived in the life of the believer (see Gal. 2:20; 4:19; 1 John 4:12).

Paul's goal was to bring into maturity and adulthood all those who had faith in Jesus Christ (see Col. 1:28). This required labor and conflict. But it is the power of God that will work out this kind of teaching, if God calls you into such a ministry. "This is my work, and I can do it only because Christ's mighty energy is at work within me" (Col. 1:29, *TLB*). Are you called to this kind of ministry? Your church needs teachers; your neighborhood, your home, your business gives you opportunity. Are you looking for these opportunities, trusting God for the power that works mightily in you, and obediently obeying God's plan for your life?

Paul said that he could "rejoice in my suffering for you" (Col. 1:24, *KJV*). He said he became a servant of the Church when God made him responsible for delivering God's message to the Colossians (see Col. 1:25). His life became an example in his circumstances for the Christians whom he had never met but loved very much because of their faith in Christ.

There is a saying, "Do as I say, not as I do." Paul did not live by this example. The Ontario Health Minister, when being sworn into office, announced that he was in complete agreement with the former health minister in demanding a complete ban on cigarette advertising. While making the statement, he lit a cigarette and said, "But, that's not going to stop me from smoking." That's a case of "Do as I say, not as I do." But example is stronger than words, and if those in responsible Christian positions do not set the right example, others will measure their lives by this example. The Colossians could measure their lives by Paul's example of rejoicing in his sufferings for their sake. Are you this kind of an example? Our lives constantly manifest what we truly think of Christ.

GROW IN HIS WISDOM AND KNOWLEDGE
COLOSSIANS 2

Before you begin your study this week:
1. Pray and ask God to speak to you through His Holy Spirit each day.
2. Use only your Bible for your answers.
3. Write your answers and the verses you have used.
4. Challenge questions are for those who have the time and wish to do them.
5. Personal questions are to be shared with your study group only if you wish to share.
6. As you study, look for a verse to memorize this week. Write it down, carry it with you, tack it to your bulletin board, tape it to the dashboard of your car. Make a real effort to learn the verse and its reference.

FIRST DAY: Read all of Colossians 2 concentrating on verses 1,2.

1. Paul had great conflict, or we could say he was strenuously praying for the Colossian Christians (see Col. 1:3, 9-11). What other Christians was he anxious enough about to be strenuously praying for them?

2. (Personal) Do you love your fellow Christians enough to pray for them? Do you ever pray for Christians you have never seen, yet are anxious for? List and share some examples to encourage others.

103

3. How did Paul pray that these Christians' hearts could be "comforted" or "encouraged?" (see Col. 2:2).

4. **Challenge:** There is to be unity and brotherly love among those who have faith in Jesus Christ. What do the following verses teach about this? If you wish, put your own name into these verses and personalize them to challenge yourself to trust God to work out this love through your life toward other Christians.

   John 13:35

   2 Corinthians 13:11

   1 Peter 3:8

5 a. (Personal) Which of these verses was the most challenging to you? Will you pray and ask God for His help in any area where you feel weak as a Christian and need God, and by the power of the Holy Spirit to help you in relationships with others?

   b. We cannot love anyone properly and kindly with understanding and compassion. Mere humans are incapable of this, but by faith in Christ we receive the gift of the Holy Spirit (see Eph. 1:12-14) who empowers us to love other people with Christlike love. Romans 5:5 explains this very clearly. Write down this verse and claim it for yourself.

c. (Personal) Think of someone you cannot love by human **strength**. Now make an experiment in faith! Begin each day to pray that God will give you a Christlike love for this person, according to His promise in Romans 5:5.

6. **Challenge:** Paul wanted his fellow Christians to have full knowledge of God's mystery in Christ (see Col. 2:2). A mystery in the Scriptures is a previously hidden truth now revealed by God. Read 1 Timothy 3:16 (using the *King James Version* and a modern language translation) to discover the "mystery" revealed by God, which Paul wanted Christians to fully understand—so that their hearts would be "fully comforted" by this knowledge. What do you believe the mystery is that Paul speaks of in Colossians 2:2?

SECOND DAY: Read Colossians 2:3-7.

1. What treasures does Christ have to give the Christian?

2 a. **Challenge:** The following Scriptures foretell, or tell, of Christ's treasures of wisdom and knowledge. What do you learn about these treasures? Use your own words if you wish to.

Isaiah 11:2

Isaiah 33:6

Romans 11:33

b. (Personal) Which of these verses brought you a new thought about Jesus Christ, or reminded you of the wonderful wisdom and knowledge available to Christians through Christ the Lord?

3 a. What is Paul's concern for Christians? (see Col. 2:4).

b. How does Romans 16:17,18 warn all Christians to be careful about those who go against what the Bible teaches?

4 a. What did Paul urge Christians to do in Colossians 2:6?

b. (Personal) Have you received Christ Jesus yet? (see 2 Cor. 6:2). If so, how are you sharing Him with others and walking in Him?

5. According to the following verses, how can Christians walk in Christ?

   Colossians 2:7

   Ephesians 3:17

6. How do you believe God's Word in 2 Timothy 2:15 and 3:16 can help you walk in Christ? Put your thoughts into your own words if you wish to.

THIRD DAY: Read Colossians 2:8-13.

1. Paul warned of false religions in Colossians 2:8. How does he describe them?

2. God gives us the remedy for being taken in by false religions, and this remedy centers in Jesus Christ. What do you learn about Jesus Christ in Colossians 2:9 and 10?

3. What does John 1:14 say about Jesus Christ?

4. Which verse in Colossians 2 speaks of Christ's resurrection? Give the phrase in the verse that mentions this.

5. Which verse says that people are dead in sin before they come by faith to Jesus Christ, who forgives these trespasses?

6 a. What does Hebrews 12:1,2 encourage every Christian to do?

   b. (Personal) Will you take up the challenge God gives you in Hebrews 12:1,2? Why not pray about this now? What does Hebrews 12:3 instruct the Christian to do?

FOURTH DAY: Read Colossians 2:14-19.

1. First Peter 2:24 contains similar concepts found in Colossians 2:14. What does 1 Peter 2:24 say?

2. **Challenge:** What similar thoughts do you find about Christ's death on the cross in Colossians 2:14 and 1 Peter 2:24?

3. By Christ's death we receive God's gracious forgiveness through His sacrifice on the cross, and the Christian's debt is cancelled through faith in Jesus Christ, the Lord (see Col. 2:14). Over what did Christ triumph, according to Colossians 2:15?

4. **Challenge:** How does Ephesians 1:19-22 express God's triumphant power shown in Christ? List these points by verse. Example: 1. Verse 19—Power to those who believe.

5. In Colossians 2:16-19, Paul, led by the Holy Spirit, warned the Colossian Christians not to be led astray by false teachers. Choose a few of the things that he warns against and list them with the verse.

6. God is warning all Christians in Colossians 2:16-18 of deceivers who would seek to take a Christian away from the simplicity of the gospel—good news—of Jesus Christ. How do the following verses warn against the same thing? Summarize these verses in your own words.

    Romans 16:17,18

    2 Corinthians 11:13-15

FIFTH DAY: Read Colossians 2:20-23.

1. The Holy Spirit led Paul to say that man's rules and regulations only "satisfy the flesh" or "make a man proud" and are of "no real value in controlling physical passions." He goes on in Colossians 3 to give the way a Christian should live. Read Romans 8, which relates somewhat to Colossians 3. Choose some verses that are

meaningful to you and share them with the class. Write them in your own words.

2. Review the verse in this lesson that you memorized this week. Write the verse and its reference and keep it along with others you have learned in an accessible place so you can easily review your verses and grow in your spiritual treasure chest.

SIXTH DAY: Read all the Notes and look up the Scriptures.

1. What new thought did you find helpful in the Notes?

2. What personal application did you select to apply to your own life this week?

Study Notes

Paul's emotions were involved in tense conflict—which in the Greek meant "agony"—because of the demonic opposition directed against God's truth (see 1 Tim. 4:1-5; 1 John 4:1-4). This spiritual struggle that Paul was involved in was for God's people at Colosse and Laodicea. He said, "I wish you could understand how deep is my anxiety for you, and for those at Laodicea, and for all who have never met me. How I long that they may be encouraged, and find out more and more how strong are the bonds of Christian love. How I long for them to experience the wealth of conviction which is brought by understanding—that they may come to know more fully God's great secret, Christ himself! For it is *in him*, and in him alone, that men will find all the treasures of wisdom and knowledge. I write like this to prevent you from being led astray by someone or other's attractive arguments. For though I am a long way from you in body, in spirit I am by your side, rejoicing as I see the solid steadfastness of your faith in Christ" (Col. 2:1-5, *Phillips*).

Christ Is the Answer to Doctrinal Error Colossians 2:1-7

Paul used words such as *wisdom* and *knowledge*, which were dear to the Gnostics, and turned them into effective instruments of Christian truth. The Gnostics taught that angels were mediating beings between man and God, and that there was redemption through the knowledge that men could attain for themselves. Paul made it plain in this letter that the Gnostic teaching was not truth: "*For God's secret plan, now at last made known, is Christ himself.* In him lie hidden all the mighty, untapped treasures of wisdom and knowledge" (Col. 2:2,3, *TLB*).

> **The world's richest people are those who have the knowledge of God's mystery revealed in Christ.**

We see Paul's personal concern for the church at Colosse and Laodicea as he longed for these Christians to be established and kept firm in their convictions. He did not want the shrewd philosophers and legalists of their day to deceive these Christians. The best way to be protected from the snares of the world and its philosophy is an understanding of the perfection of Christ for "Christ is all, and in all" (Col. 3:11, *NASB*).

We Need to Be Rooted and Grounded in His Word

Paul wanted these Christians to be rooted and grounded in the Word of God so they would not be swept away by false teachers. He wanted them to understand that Christ was the only way to the Father (see John 14:6), and that Christ was the only mediator between God and man. "Since you have received, don't be deceived!" seemed to be the essence of Paul's counsel here.

In Colossians 2:2 Paul spoke of the "riches of assured understanding and the knowledge of God's mystery, of Christ" (*RSV*). Most people in the secular world believe that money brings peace, satisfaction and security. Of course it doesn't! The world's richest people are those who have the knowledge of God's mystery revealed in Christ. This mystery is God's secret plan made long ago, and now at last made known in the appearance of the living Lord Jesus Christ. In other words, if there was a secret, Paul said that Christ was it! Christ who is God Himself came in the flesh from His heavenly home to give His life on the cross that man might be forgiven his sins and reconciled to God through Christ's sacrifice. "And He Himself bore our sins in His body on the cross, that we might die to sin and live to righteousness; for by His wounds you were healed" (1 Pet. 2:24, *NASB*).

We Need to Encourage Fellow Believers

Paul's purpose was to encourage Christians and unite them in love. The one mark that distinguishes a true church is love for God and love for fellow Christians. When love is there, the church is strong because Jesus Christ, the Lord of love, is there.

The reason for such love is given by the Lord Himself. "By this shall all men know that ye are my disciples, if ye have love one to another" (John 13:35, *KJV*). This is the identifying badge of the Christian. The early church flashed its badge of love and had a tremendous impact upon their generation. Have you answered this command of the Lord? (see John 15:12). Is your life characterized by love, or do others only see petty jealousy, pride, self-centeredness and bickering? Some Christian educators have indicated that children from seemingly good Christian homes become indifferent because they see a gap between what is practiced in the home and what is shown to acquaintances and church members. Could this be true in your family?

How can we demonstrate a kind of spiritual love and real concern for one another in practical ways just as Christ planned for us to do? We must realize we can't exhibit such love by self-effort for God's love is the fruit of the Holy Spirit (see Gal. 5:22) and it comes from God (see 1 John 4:7,10). The Lord Jesus Christ prayed that God's love would be injected into the Christian's personality. "And I have declared unto them thy name, and will declare it: that the love wherewith thou hast loved me may be in them, and I in them" (John 17:26, *KJV*). The more consistently we yield our lives to Jesus Christ the more the love fruit of the Holy Spirit will begin to glow and flow throughout our personality.

> We are the only Bibles the careless world will read;
> We are the sinner's Gospel; we are the scoffer's creed;
> We are the Lord's last message, given in deed and word;
> What if the type is crooked, what if the print is blurred?
> —Anonymous

Are You Walking and Growing in the Lord?

Paul's desire was that these Christians should continue to walk and live with Christ Jesus as they had begun in faith. "As ye have therefore received Christ Jesus the Lord, so walk ye in him: rooted and built up in him" (Col. 2:6,7, *KJV*). Paul was always practical. Again he said, "Act out what you believe. Ye have commenced well, go on as you have begun!" Paul wanted all Christians' walk and life to correspond with their beliefs. It is sad when a Christian believes in Christ, but does not act according to that belief. No one will accept his faith as sincere. If you have received Jesus Christ as your Lord and Savior, walk as He would have you walk! If you have been rooted in Him, grow up in Him! This means that you will mature in your faith through the study of God's Word and prayer time spent with Him.

An example of walking and growing is exhibited in the life of a famous baseball manager, Al Dark. He states, "Many times during my baseball managing years at Cleveland I got down on my knees and prayed, asking for guidance, but I never got into the Word of God or did what God said. Now it's a natural thing for me to sit and read the Bible. The difference, I think, is this: a dedicated Christian who is depending on the Lord has to go to the Bible to find out what the Lord wants him to do, so he can do it."

He goes on to state, "One day in Baltimore before a game, my wife and I were in the hotel room, studying about Christ on the cross. We read how He was spat upon and mocked, and how He suffered. That night I went to the ballpark and about the eighth or ninth inning, after taking one of my pitchers out of the game, I was stepping out of the dugout when an angry fan threw beer in my face. Well, in the years before this I would have been over the dugout to get him; but because we had been studying the Bible, how Christ was spat upon for me, I simply wiped away the beer from my face. I didn't even look up. The Word of God is what keeps me on an even keel. It brings me right back to my knees."

Al Dark's life expresses walking and growing as he has studied the Bible and spent time in prayer. Are you willing to take the time for these things so Colossians 2:6,7 may become a growing experience in your life?

We have to do a great deal more than just believe truths about Christ. We must receive Christ if we are to have life (see John 14:6). We cannot earn it or purchase it. It is a free gift (see Col. 2:6; Eph. 2:8-10). A Christian needs to be rooted in Christ, which means he draws his nourishment from Him. A plant cannot grow unless it is in touch with the life-giving soil. We have our foundation in Christ. Every structure needs a foundation. All this must be our experience if we would be "built up."

> **Thanksgiving should be the constant and characteristic note of the Christian life!**

When a French housewife rushed out one day to get to the market before it closed, she slammed the front door of her house behind her. To her astonishment the entire house collapsed! Later she explained, "The main beam had been loose for years, but workmen were too busy to come to repair it." The "main beam" of a Christian's life needs to be "built on the solid rock" of the Lord Jesus Christ. The Lord Jesus spoke of a man who built his house upon the sand; and when the storms arose, the house fell, "And great was the fall of it" (Matt. 7:27, KJV).

We Are Wise to Listen

Christ said, "All who listen to my instructions and follow them are wise, like a man who builds his house on solid rock. Though the rain comes in torrents, and the floods rise and the storm winds beat against his house, it won't collapse, for it is built on rock" (Matt. 7:24,25 TLB). Have you built the foundation of your life upon this strong and sure rock, Jesus Christ? (see 1 Cor. 10:4). "As you have therefore received Christ Jesus the Lord, so walk ye in him" (Col. 2:6, KJV).

Before leaving this section there is one phrase in Colossians 2:7 well worth thinking about: "Overflowing with gratitude" or "abounding therein with thanksgiving." Paul stressed our thankfulness to the Lord in several places in Colossians (see 1:12; 3:15). Thanksgiving should be the constant and characteristic note of the Christian life! "Thanksgiving is the end of all human conduct, whether observed in words or works" (J.B. Lightfoot). Are you thankful? Do you praise God in word and deed for all that He has done for you?

The Dangers of False Philosophy Colossians 2:8-13

"Don't let others spoil your faith and joy with their philosophies, their wrong and shallow answers built on men's thoughts and ideas, instead of on what Christ has said. For in Christ there is all of God in a human body; *so you have everything when you have Christ,* and you are filled with God through your union with Christ. He is the highest Ruler, with authority over every other power" (Col. 2:8-10, *TLB*). There was a philosophy being taught—the love of knowledge—and this placed the Christian in danger of being encouraged to consider Christ's work on the cross as rather unimportant. Such "vain systems of thought" had been built up and handed down by unbelieving men and were not "of Christ" (see Col. 2:8).

These false teachers wished the Colossians to accept "additions to Christ." They were teaching that Jesus Christ Himself was not sufficient, not unique, and that He was one among many manifestations of God. They taught that it was necessary to worship other so-called divine and angelic powers in addition to Christ.

There were others who wished to impose circumcision on Christians (see Col. 2:11). They said that faith was not enough. This practice had to be added to it. A badge in the flesh was to take the place of, or at least be in addition to, the attitude of the heart. Paul spoke of the "circumcision made without hands," which referred to the Church as God's true temple brought into faith by Christ's death and resurrection (see Heb. 9:11-14; Rom. 3:30). "We are truly circumcised when we worship God by the Spirit; we pride ourselves in Jesus Christ and put no confidence in the flesh" (Phil. 3:3, *Phillips*).

Thus we see that there was a mixture of Gnosticism and Judaism being taught the Christians at Colosse. The Gnostics taught the necessity of intellectual knowledge, philosophy and worship of angels, in addition to faith in Christ as a necessity for a Christian. The teachings went beyond the message needed for salvation (see John 3:16,17). Those who wanted to impose circumcision as a part of the

Christian faith also wanted to lay down other rules and regulations (see Col. 2:16,18,20-23). They wanted the Christians to follow rules and regulations about what they could eat and drink, and what days they could observe certain festivals and fasts. All of the old Jewish food laws and all of the old Jewish regulations were to be brought back and added to them.

Paul pointed out to those Christians that the remedy for all of the false religious teachings was in Christ and in adherence to the truth of His full deity in humanity—perfect God-perfect Man (see John 1:14; Col. 1:19). Paul said, "Ye are complete in him, which is the head of all principality and power" (Col. 2:10, *KJV*). In Colossians 2:11 he spoke of "circumcision made without hands" referring to the "mark" of Christ within the life of the believer when they put off the body of the sins of the flesh. "When you came to Christ he set you free from your evil desires, not by a bodily operation of circumcision but by a spiritual operation, the baptism of your souls" (Col. 2:11, *TLB*).

In Baptism We Are Buried with Christ

Paul said, "Having been buried with him in baptism and raised with him through your faith in the power of God, who raised him from the dead" (Col. 2:12, *NIV*). This baptism may primarily refer to Christ's baptism of death (see Mark 10:38; Luke 12:50), although Christian baptism is not to be excluded. "Have you forgotten that all of us who were baptized into Jesus Christ were, by that very action, sharing in his death? We were dead and buried with him in baptism, so that just as he was raised from the dead by that splendid revelation of the Father's power so we too might rise to life on a new plane altogether" (Rom. 6:3,4, *Phillips*).

Colossians 2 verses 11-13 are interpreted differently by Bible commentators. The main thoughts we can agree upon here are that a Christian must believe in the effective working of God and His power that raised Jesus Christ from the dead (see Col. 2:12). Only then can you be convinced that the power that brought Jesus Christ through the cross and raised Him in the resurrection can do the same for you.

Paul used the word *baptism* for the Christian to symbolize dying to old sins and ways of life and rising again to a new life, trusting the Word of the mighty God who raised Christ from the dead. "You were dead in sins, and your sinful desires were not yet cut away. Then he gave you a share in the very life of Christ, for he forgave all your sins" (Col. 2:13, *TLB*).

Have you been on the receiving end of God's forgiveness? Are you helping others to realize the joy in sharing the life of Christ and forgiveness of their sins?

Our Salvation Is Free! Colossians 2:14-17

When the veil of the Temple was ripped from top to bottom at Christ's death, the end of the legal age was indicated (see Matt. 27:51; Luke 23:45; Heb. 9:3-8; 10:19,20). Christ had fulfilled the law and by His death He had liberated us from its condemnation (see Matt. 5:17). "He forgave us all our sins, having canceled the written code, with its regulations, that was against us and that stood opposed to us; he took it away, nailing it to the cross" (Col. 2:13,14, *NIV*; see also Eph. 2:15,16). Christ also defeated Satanic and demonic powers, which were binding us (see Eph. 6:12; Heb. 2:14) and made a public spectacle of them in His triumph. "In this way God took away Satan's power to accuse you of sin, and God openly displayed to the whole world Christ's triumph at the cross where your sins were all taken away" (Col. 2:15, *TLB*).

Because of Christ's full emancipation, the Christian believer should not pass judgment upon another believer in matters of food, observance of festival days, which the Jewish people had practiced concerning holy days, the new moon and the Sabbath day. The Christian is complete in Christ and has been accepted by Him, therefore no fellow Christian is to reject such a believer because he does not observe such legal customs. These legal ceremonies were only types or shadows of the real things to come in Christ Jesus. Therefore, these customs neither add nor subtract from the completeness the believer in Christ Jesus enjoys in Him. "And ye are complete in him, which is the head of all principality and power" (Col. 2:10, *KJV*).

There are those today who would impose their own customs upon other Christians and rob them of their completeness in Jesus Christ. A true story is told of an elderly woman who spoke with feeling about her love for Christ, but she lacked an assurance of her faith and spiritual joy. She had a serious heart ailment and was afraid of death. She spent much time in Bible reading and prayer, and without her husband's knowledge had given large sums of money to her denomination. She said hopefully, "I did this for my salvation." She confided all these things to a Christian friend who gently called her attention to Paul's declaration that, "If righteousness come by the law, then Christ is dead in vain" (Gal. 2:21, *KJV*). She reminded her that no amount of good works would be enough to earn her way to heaven. Even her best deeds were tainted by a certain amount of selfishness and pride. She readily agreed, for she had a feeling of guilt about the money she had secretly given her church.

The friend reminded her that only when she trusted completely in Christ, rather than rely upon her own imperfect acts of obedience to God, could she have a peace to know that God would accept her as she was, forgive her sins and give her the gift of eternal life. "For by grace you have been saved through faith; and this is not your own doing, it is the gift of God—not because of works, lest any man should boast" (Eph. 2:8,9, *RSV*). Paul told us in Colossians 2:13,14, "You were dead in sins, and your sinful desires were not yet cut away. Then he gave you a share in the very life of Christ, for he forgave all your sins, and blotted out the charges proved against you, the list of his commandments which you had not obeyed. He took this list of sins and destroyed it by nailing it to Christ's cross" (*TLB*). Are you resting completely in Jesus Christ? He is the only basis for your assurance and peace.

Beware of False Teaching Colossians 2:18-23

Paul posed a very interesting question with its own answer in Colossians 2:20-23. "If, through your faith in Christ, you are dead to the principles of this world's life, why, as if you were still part and parcel of this world-wide system, do you take the slightest notice of these purely human prohibitions—'Don't touch this;' 'Don't taste that,' and 'Don't handle the other'? 'This,' 'that' and 'the other' will all pass away after use! I know that these regulations look wise with their self-inspired efforts at piety, their policy of self-humbling, and their studied neglect of the body. But in actual practice they are of no moral value, but simply pamper the flesh" (*Phillips*).

Paul pointed out that the world had its own ideas about righteousness and goodness. Man says, "I want to do it my way." When we are joined to Jesus Christ by faith we have God's righteousness. Paul was saying to be severed from the world and don't become involved in its ways, for those ways can sever your fellowship with Christ. If you died with Christ to the basic principles of this world, why, as though you still belong to it, do you submit to its rules? (see Col. 2:20).

The Christian is to take the position that he is dead to any form of legalism and therefore is delivered from legalistic do's and don'ts (see Rom. 6:11). The result of this emancipation by Christ is that we can as Christians be led by the Holy Spirit and our lives can be used for God as He intended! (see Acts 5:32; Rom. 5:5; 1 Cor. 2:4,10).

We Are Joined Together in Christ

In closing this lesson, let us consider Colossians 2:19 from the *The Living Bible*, which describes the false teachers in Colosse who were trying to indoctrinate the Colossian Christians with erroneous teachings: "But they are not connected to Christ, the Head to which all of us who are his body are joined; for we are joined together by his strong sinews and we grow only as we get our nourishment and strength from God."

Paul anguished and struggled in prayer and concern for these Christians that they would not be deceived by false teachings. He wrote this letter to those believers in Colosse and Laodicea and other areas so that they might know the truth about Jesus Christ, God's only Son.

Paul said in Galatians 2:20, "I have been crucified with Christ: and I myself no longer live, but Christ lives in me. And the real life I now have within this body is a result of my trusting in the Son of God, who loved me and gave himself for me" (*TLB*). Paul didn't care about his own life. He only cared that his fellow Christians would grow in their faith and love for Jesus Christ!

Heart Hunters for Jesus

In 1839 John Williams, who was called the apostle of the South Seas, and another missionary by the name of Harris sailed to the New Hebrides. After a period of service, they were clubbed to death by savages. Eighteen years later, G.N. Gordon and his wife went to the same islands and were killed. Mr. Gordon's brother went to the same place and was killed in 1872. Later, two missionaries named Tanner and Nesbit went to one of the many islands of this group and stayed for seven months. Finally, however, they had to flee for their lives by night in an open boat.

John G. Paton felt that God was calling him to these islands, and when he told a friend of his plans, the friend replied, "You'll be eaten by cannibals!" Paton replied, "Mr. Dickson, you are old—soon you will be put into the grave and your body eaten by worms. But if I can live and die serving the Lord Jesus Christ, it doesn't make any difference to me whether I'm eaten by cannibals or worms."

Paton left on his dangerous, God-appointed mission. He learned the language of the people and won many to Christ. What a thrill it must have been for him when he held his first communion service with 12 Christian natives. He said, "I shall never taste a deeper bliss until I gaze on the glorified face of Jesus Himself!" Paton lived to see 16,000 South Sea islanders sing of God's love. Now on the plains where savages once killed and ate each other, there are Christian churches, schools and printing presses!

Is God Calling You?

Who is God calling you to care about? God called Paul to care about many Christians, some he knew personally and some he never saw.

God called Williams, Gordon, Tanner, Nesbit and finally Paton to vicious headhunters so that they might have a knowledge of God's mercy and love expressed in Jesus Christ His only Son! Do you listen long enough each day to hear God's Word and His call to you? In God's eyes it is a great thing to do a little thing well, when He calls you to do it!

CHRIST IS ALL-SUFFICIENT
COLOSSIANS 3

Before you begin your study this week:
1. Pray and ask God to speak to you through His Holy Spirit each day.
2. Use only your Bible for your answers.
3. Write your answers and the verses you have used.
4. Challenge questions are for those who have the time and wish to do them.
5. Personal questions are to be shared with your study group only if you wish to share.
6. As you study, look for a verse to memorize this week. Write it down, carry it with you, tack it to your bulletin board, tape it to the dashboard of your car. Make a real effort to learn the verse and its reference.

FIRST DAY: Read all of Colossians 3 concentrating on verses 1-4.

1. How does Romans 8:11 help you understand Paul's statement concerning the Christian in Colossians 3:1—for example, "If ye be risen with Christ" or "Since you became alive again, so to speak, when Christ rose from the dead"?

2. How does Galatians 2:20 further help you understand the phrase from Colossians 3:1 given in question 1, and help you understand Colossians 3:3?

3 a. How does 2 Corinthians 5:17 describe how the Holy Spirit, who comes to live or "abide" within the Christian, affects a change in the life of the new Christian?

b. What does Colossians 3:2 say a Christian should do?

c. (Personal) What do you value and think of more—God's interests or your interests? If you can think of a specific instance where the Holy Spirit living within you has changed an earthly attitude to God's point of view, share it with your class.

4 a. The Christian who has died to selfish desires, values and judgments now sees things as they appear to God and has God's standard of values (see Col. 3:3). How is this Christian's life described in Colossians 3:3?

b. **Challenge:** Summarize the thoughts of 2 Corinthians 5:14,15 and how they complement and are similar to Colossians 3:2,3. Use your own words if you wish, and add your name to these verses.

5 a. Colossians 3:4 tells us that Christ is "life." What does John 14:6 tell you about life?

b. (Personal) It is probably John 14:6 that inspired the One Way Christian stickers, pins and signs young Christians often use. Have you invited Jesus Christ into your life? He is the only way to the Father (see Acts 3:19).

6. What promise do you find for Christians in Colossians 3:4?

SECOND DAY: Read Colossians 3:5-9.

1. **Challenge:** Colossians 3:5 points out that the Christian is to put to death bodily actions and attitudes that are not Christlike. In other words, the Christian is to put to death or to quit every action or thought that keeps him from loving and serving God. The following verses help us to more fully understand Colossians 3:5 and explain the sad results of a pleasure seeking life. What does each verse teach?

   Luke 8:14—Spiritual barrenness;

   James 5:1-6—Worldly goals. Summarize the thoughts of this passage and give the verse. (Example: Verse 1. There are terrible troubles ahead for rich men who have oppressed people. Verse 2. Your wealth is rotting away and your fine clothes have become moth-eaten.)

2. List all of the "works of the flesh" that are to be avoided. They are named in Colossians 3:5-9. (Example: Verse 5. Immorality—fornication; Verse 5. Impurity—uncleanness.)

3. How does Ephesians 5:6,7 help you understand Colossians 3:6?

4. It is not necessary to live in a selfish, self-willed existence if the Christian will trust the Holy Spirit to produce the good fruit of God in his life. What does Galatians 5:16 say about this?

5. Read Galatians 5:22,23 and list the fruit of the Spirit. Then read Galatians 5:24,25 and list the principles for Christian living.

Galatians 5:22,23

Galatians 5:24,25

6. (Personal) Have you ever asked God for the power and fruit of the Holy Spirit? Why not pray now about this? Is there a fruit missing in your life? Ask God to give it to you as you promise "to walk in the Spirit" and follow the Holy Spirit's guidance each day.

THIRD DAY: Read Colossians 3:10-15.

1. When a person becomes a Christian, there ought to be some changes in his personality and behavior. How does Colossians 3:10 describe this?

2. In this new life that Christ gives to Christians by the power of the Holy Spirit, one's nationality, race and education is unimportant (see Col. 3:11). What *is* important according to Colossians 3:11?

3. What do you discover from reading Colossians 3:12-14 that Christian should put on and practice in the new life?

4. (Personal) If possible reread Colossians 3:12-14 in several Bible translations and paraphrases. Do you need to pray and ask God to help you in a particular area that should be a part of your Christian life?

5. Do you know a Christian who is an illustration of some of these qualities God gives by His Holy Spirit? Share, without mentioning names, how you have seen or experienced one of the qualities

mentioned in Colossians 3:12-14. Perhaps you have watched or been a part of the life and love of Christ expressed through such a Christian. It is good to share such joys!

6. What two things should all Christians have as they are one body by faith in Christ Jesus?

FOURTH AND FIFTH DAYS: Read Colossians 3:16-25.

1 a. What does Colossians 3:16,17 encourage each Christian to do?

b. How does 1 Timothy 4:11,12 add to the thought of Christians teaching Christ's words and truths to others, as mentioned in Colossians 3:16?

c. (Personal) Meditate on Colossians 3:16 and 1 Timothy 4:11,12. Is there some particular area you would like to pray about so God could increase your influence as a Christian?

2. Colossians 3:18-21 deals with Christian family life. List the concepts given and give each verse.

3. **Challenge:** How do the following verses help to enlarge your thoughts on God's plan for a happy family?

Exodus 20:12

Ephesians 5:21-25

1 Peter 3:1

4. What do you believe Colossians 3:21 means? If possible give some illustrations without using names.

5 a. Whether we work at home or are out in the business world, what should our attitudes be as Christians? (see Col. 3:22-24).

   b. **Challenge:** It is Christ who will give the Christian his "inheritance" or "the full portion of all Christ owns" (see Col. 3:24). Read 1 Peter 1:3,4. How does this help you understand what your inheritance is as a Christian?

6. Which verse did you choose to memorize for encouragement this week? Write it down with the reference.

SIXTH DAY: Read all the Notes and look up the Scriptures.

1. What new thought did you find helpful in the Notes?

2. What personal application did you select to apply to your own life this week?

Study Notes

In Colossians 2 we learned that we must depend upon Christ for a faithful walk in our Christian life and for our assurance of salvation. "And you yourselves, who were strangers to God, and, in fact, through the evil things you have done, his spiritual enemies, he has now reconciled through the death of Christ's body on the cross, so that he might welcome you to his presence clean and pure, without blame or reproach" (Col. 1:20-22, Phillips). Yes, all the life we have as Christians is the life in Him!

1. Walk in Him (see Col. 2:6)
2. Rooted in Him (see Col. 2:7)
3. Built up in Him (see Col. 2:7)
4. Brought to perfection in Him (see Col. 2:10)
5. Dead with Him (see Col. 2:20)
6. Risen with Him (see Col. 3:1)
7. Hidden with Him (see Col. 3:3)

This is the life—real and satisfying, eternal life! We find that Christ is all sufficient for "In him dwelleth all the fulness of the Godhead bodily" (Col. 2:9, *KJV*)—perfect God-perfect Man.

Focus for the Christian Life Colossians 3:1-4

The building of our life should not only be downward—"rooted in Christ" (see Col. 2:7) and upward—"built up in Him" (see Col. 2:7), but it must also be "inward." The life that is in Christ is in the believer! Jesus Christ gave this illustration in John 15:5: "I am the vine, ye are the branches" (*KJV*). We find that our new life in Christ makes us less interested in the things the world offers. "Set your minds on things above, not on earthly things" (Col. 3:2, *NIV*). We become "dead to the world" and see things not as they appear to men but as they appear to God. We find ourselves "hid with Christ in God" (Col. 3:3). As we know Him we discover, one by one, the beauties of the Lord Jesus Christ.

Since the Christian is rooted in Christ and his life is hid in Christ, he is not only identified with Christ's death, but also is in union with Christ in His resurrection. In Christ's death we died to sin, and in His resurrection we rose to walk in a new life. Since we are risen with Christ, we should seek things that are above (see Col. 3:2), and show to the best of our ability the goals of our lives. We live in the world, but we must set our minds on things above, for we are citizens of a heavenly country. "Now all of us, whether Jews or Gentiles, may come to God the Father with the Holy Spirit's help because of what Christ has done for us. Now you are no longer strangers to God and foreigners to heaven, but you are members of God's very own family, citizens of God's country, and you belong in God's household with every other Christian" (Eph. 2:18,19, *TLB*).

> *In Christ's death we died to sin, and in His resurrection we rose to walk in a new life.*

The Lord Jesus tells us to set our hearts on the things that are above and also to store for ourselves treasures in heaven, noting that "where your treasure is, there will your heart be also" (Matt. 6:21, *KJV*). If we shift our investments to heaven, we soon have so much laid up there that our hearts cannot be any other place!

A letter in the *San Diego Evening Tribune* began, "Dear Thief, We have so much stuff in the garage that we could not tell what it was you took." The owner of the garage spotted a man stealing something heavy from her garage, but she could not make out a report to the police because she did not know what was stolen! "Until we finally miss what it was you took, we can't report it missing," she wrote. "If we can't report it stolen, we can't claim our loss and deduct it from our income taxes. Well, would you, just as a token of your appreciation, send us an itemized list of what you stole and its approximate value so we can turn it in to our tax man?" What a commentary on human nature! Many people have so many things that they cannot keep an inventory of what they have. Many people derive a sense of security from collections of things! How much better to lay up our treasures in heaven "where thieves do not break through nor steal" (Matt. 6:20, *KJV*).

We Shall Be Like Him

In Colossians 3:4 Paul gave to Jesus Christ one of the great titles of devotion. He called Him, Christ our life. In Philippians 1:21 he wrote, Christ means life to me. In Galatians 2:20 the Holy Spirit led him to write, "I live; yet not I, but Christ liveth in me" (*KJV*). To the Christian Jesus Christ is more important than physical life. He is life itself!

Many times we hear people say of someone else, "he lives for his work," or "sports is his life," or "music is his life," or "her family is her life." None of these things are wrong in themselves, but for a

Christian it should always be said, "Christ is his life." The Lord Jesus Christ should fill our thoughts and lives moment by moment. We need to access everything in the light of the love of the One who loved us and gave Himself for us. In the light of the cross, the world's wealth and ambition and activities are seen in their true value. Christ has delivered us from slavery to earthly things and enabled us to set our whole hearts and affections on the things above so that we will be better musicians, sportsmen, businessmen, family members and friends.

"When Christ, who is our life, shall appear, then shall ye also appear with him in glory" (Col. 3:4, *KJV*). Christ is sitting at the right hand of the Father in glory now (see Col. 3:1; Mark 16:19; Rev. 5:12). When Christ comes again the Christian will be with Him not merely in a corporate sense, but in a personally fulfilled glory! "In my opinion whatever we may have to go through now is less than nothing compared with the magnificent future God has in store for us. The whole creation is on tiptoe to see the wonderful sight of the sons of God coming into their own" (Rom. 8:18,19, *Phillips*). In a sense Christ is our life now, but when Christ is revealed, then we will be revealed with him in glory (see Col. 3:4; 2 Cor. 3:18).

The Christian's New Wardrobe Colossians 3:5-17

We must "put off" the old nature (see Col. 3:5-9). After we receive our new life by faith in Christ Jesus, we must "put off" the deeds and habits of our former life without Christ. It should not be necessary to tell Christians they need to put off things that are more like the devil than the Savior! We are to consider ourselves "dead" to such things (see Col. 3:5).

Many great religions of the world teach that the person himself must strive to put off old habits and ways, and dress up in new traditions. This is usually an impossibility, but in Christ there is power that no human has in himself to put away such things as immorality, impurity, passion, evil desires, greed, anger, wrath, slander, abusive speech from your mouth, lies and evil practices (see Col. 3:5-9). These actions of the mind and body can only be put to death by the power of the Holy Spirit. It is not necessary to live in a selfish, self-willed existence if the Christian will trust the Holy Spirit to produce the good fruit of God in his life! Are you willing to do this? "So I say, live by the Spirit, and you will not gratify the desires of the sinful nature. For the sinful nature desires what is contrary to the Spirit, and the Spirit what is contrary to the sinful nature" (Gal. 5:16,17, *NIV*).

God expects the Christian to lead a disciplined life. "You used to walk in these ways, in the life you once lived. But now you must rid yourselves of all such things" (Col. 3:7,8, *NIV*). God sees the Christian "in Christ." The Christian is encouraged to trust God by His Holy Spirit to empower him in this area of his life. According to Colossians 3:6 the "wrath of God will come" to those who refuse to discipline their lives in these areas. Ephesians 5:6,7 puts it this way, "Let no one deceive you with empty words, for because of such things God's wrath comes on those who are disobedient. Therefore do not be partners with them" (*NIV*).

Luciano Pavarotti is often described by his admirers as "the new Caruso." In an interview with the *T.V. Washington Post*, the 6-foot, 300-pound tenor asked, "Do you want to know the hardest thing about being a singer? It is to sacrifice yourself every moment of your life, with not one exclusion. For example: If it is raining, don't go out; eat this; do this; sleep 10 hours a day. It is not a very free life. You cannot jump on a horse. You cannot go to swim."

> *It is the disciplined person who is really free and joyful because he is able to do what God wants him to do in the power of the Holy Spirit.*

It is amazing how some Christians imagine that they can escape God's disciplines and still be their best for God! There are all kinds of ideas like discipline is legalism, discipline is repressive, discipline leads to joylessness. The truth is that it is the disciplined person who is really free and joyful because he is able to do what God wants him to do in the power of the Holy Spirit (see Gal. 5:22-25). Are you free to do what God wants you to do?

Christianity Implies New Life

Christianity is not a series of giving up pleasures. It is a new life! As we come to know Christ better, we find that some interests no longer appeal to us. Christ adds so much to our lives that there is no room for the old interests. We learn that we lose interest in the old and become busy with the new life in Christ (see Col. 3:10). Paul, led by the Holy Spirit, told us to destroy the old nature by faith in Christ and to "put off" all its vices. We can forever give up this black catalog by Christ's power. "I can do all things through Him who strengthens me" (Phil. 4:13, *NASB*). "For it is God who is at work in you, both to will and to work for His good pleasure" (Phil. 2:13, *NASB*).

Can you imagine how ridiculous you would look if, when you went to buy a new suit you refused to take off the one you had on, but rather insisted that the new one should be tried on without "putting off the old one!" This is what many Christians try to do. They try to put on the garment of a new life over their old nature. It doesn't fit! We must lay aside sin first and then "put on" the new man. A Christian's conduct in his everyday living reveals his faith.

Paul spoke of our new nature in Christ, which is ever being renewed as we grow in the knowledge of our Lord and Savior. "Let the word of Christ richly dwell within you, with all wisdom teaching and admonishing one another with psalms and hymns and spiritual songs, singing with thankfulness in your hearts to God" (Col. 3:16, *NASB*).

But we must not become so absorbed in our privileges in Christ that we neglect our duty to our fellowman! Our knowing Christ should make us much more thoughtful of others. The new Christian not only puts away, but also adds to his life. We are encouraged to put on the excellence of this new life such as tenderness, kindness, humility, patience, forgiveness and love (see Col. 3:12-14). Yes, these are the things with which we are to adorn ourselves. Paul said all of these virtues are like pieces of clothing, all held in place by a "belt of love" (see Col. 3:14).

Be Thankful for Fellow Believers

We are told to "be thankful" (see Col. 3:15) and to have thankfulness in our hearts to God. Thankfulness promotes unity among Christians as they live together, teaching, and admonishing one another (see Col. 3:16). Peace and gratitude may be looked upon as the two sides of the golden coin of contentment.

"Let the peace of Christ rule in your hearts, to which indeed you were called in one body; and be thankful" (Col. 3:15, *NASB*). This body spoken of here is the body of Christ—all those who have faith in Him make up this body (see Rom. 12:4,5; 1 Cor. 10:17; 12:12; Eph. 2:16; 4:4).

Paul's point here seems to be that thankfulness relates directly to the preservation and promotion of peace. When we are ungrateful, disunity breaks out and we are isolated from our brothers and sisters in Christ. Paul indicated that we were to be thankful. For what? The answer surely seems to be for the other members of the body! When you find it difficult to get along with a fellow Christian in the work of the Lord, start thanking God for that person. That's Paul's antidote to hostility between Christians.

Do you know how Luther Burbank took the little wild daisy and developed it into a bloom 5 to 7 inches in diameter, and the little poppy developed into a blossom 10 inches across? So must our Christian graces be cultivated and enlarged! Too often they die for want of care. We can grow in the full stature of the fullness of Christ, for as long as we live there is something new in Christ for us to learn. We should never stop growing. And we should never stop loving our fellow Christians!

A Heavenly Walk in Personal Relationships Colossians 3:18-25

Paul's letter now became more practical and centered on personal relationships. All of the principles God led Paul to put down in Colossians 3 need to be worked out in a practical way in the life of everyday Christian relationships. God wants Christians to progress in their spiritual growth, and this particular portion of Colossians gives practical instructions for such progress, by the power of the Holy Spirit within each Christian (see Zech. 4:6).

In the second letter that Peter wrote, he referred to certain believers who lacked progress in their Christian experience, and said that they were "blind and cannot see afar off" (see 2 Pet. 1:9). He said that they had forgotten that they were purged from their old sins (see 2 Pet. 1:9). Too often, Christians have far too little apprehension of the world of spiritual reality; their vision of spiritual truth is dim. They live in a gray world where their visual perception is impaired.

These people could be compared to Josephine Mulkey who fell into liquid lye at a neighbor's home when she was 6 years old. The lye blinded her in both eyes. Recently through a cornea transplant in one eye, sight was restored to this woman who had been blind for 74 years; now she can see! And so it is for the Christian, for it is never too late for God to restore His "spiritual vision" by the Holy Spirit, and thus give each believer a visual perception of what true "life in Christ" can be. Perhaps there is something you need to stop and pray about right now. Would you like to have God restore your "spiritual sight" so that you can have a right relationship not only with God, but with your fellow believers as well? What affect has Christ had in your behavior patterns on the job, in your home, among your friends and in your community?

A Husband and Wife's Relationship

The conduct of the household was a much discussed subject among the Jewish and pagan worlds, according to some Apocryphal writings. Apparently Paul taught regularly on this topic (see Eph. 5:22-33;

Titus 2:1-10). In contrast to Jewish and pagan teachings, Paul emphasized the mutuality of rights and responsibilities. The original Greek indicates that the wives may have been lax in their marital duties. Perhaps they were asserting their new freedom in Christ and the husbands grew impatient. Bitterness can quickly control a man. And since the male is stronger, he is often tempted to abandon his humility as the head of the house and deal too harshly with the problem. Paul, led by the Holy Spirit, insisted that not only must the wife submit, but the husband must reign in love; otherwise bitterness will result, which damages a marriage.

Since unity in Christ does not negate the diversity of function and status in the world (see Col. 3:11), the Christian man and woman should have a concern for proper social order and custom. The Christian husband and wife must be motivated by their relationship to Christ and responsibilities to God. God created man and woman and has endowed each sex with its peculiar functions and gifts. Within each He has allowed for differences of personality, temperament, ability, intelligence and shape. There are some women who are more skilled carpenters and administrators than some men, while there are some men who are better kindergarten teachers or cooks than women!

Christians need to follow the pattern set down in the Bible concerning our life and particularly here in Colossians 3:18, 19 concerning the relationship of the wife to the husband. A wife's submission is to be reciprocated in the husband's love. The love here does not merely mean affection, but an outgoing concern for the wife's whole person.

We need to live by God's principles if we are to find real happiness and fulfillment in this life. There is a familiar old story of the lady who crossed the ocean with a ticket purchased for her by her son. The woman had prepared for herself a very large lunch to eat on the journey. Toward the end of her trip the milk was sour, the bread was dry, the butter was rancid, and the fruit was completely decayed. To top it all off, just before landing she found out that her ticked had included all first-class meals at the captain's table! Due to ignorance she had starved herself.

Many Christians are like this: hungry, unhappy and defeated. They struggle along when they might be feeding on the best of the king's table. People are often ignorant of the rich supply in God's treasure house, the Bible (see Col. 2:3).

Failure to feed on the Word of God regularly and systematically will result in irreparable loss. Why not take time to read God's menu? The truths and promises of Scripture may be compared to fragrant flowers—meditation like the bees who sip the honey out of them! (see Ps. 19:7-11).

What Is the Parent's Duty?

Colossians 3:20,21 deals with children and parents. God holds the parents responsible for the maturity of their children. Disobedient children displease the Lord, even as do the parents who tolerate them. If the parent is too easygoing, the child grows up undisciplined and unfit to face life. "Children, obey your parents in all things: for this is well pleasing unto the Lord" (Col. 3:20, *KJV*). Conversely, there is a danger of over-correcting a child. God says, "Fathers, do not exasperate your children, that they may not lose heart" (Col. 3:21, *NASB*).

Mary Lamb said, "Why is it that I never seem able to do anything to please my mother?" John Newton was quoted as saying, "I know that my father loved me—but he did not seem to wish me to see it." The danger in this type of treatment is that the child becomes discouraged and very often has a broken spirit. A parent's duty is not only to discipline but to encourage as well.

One of the tragic facts of religious history is that Martin Luther's father was so stern with him that all his days Luther found it difficult to pray "Our Father." The word *father* in his mind stood for nothing but severity. The duty of a Christian parent is to discipline and encourage. Luther himself said, "Spare the rod and spoil the child. It is true. But beside the rod, keep an apple to give him when he does well."

Service with a Smile

The final verses of Colossians 3 deal with the relationship of slaves to their masters. In Paul's day, slaves were cruelly exploited. Yet today these verses can apply to modern employees. Christians can endure low wages and hard conditions, and still give sincere service with a smile.

The Christian needs to consider his real "boss" who is the Lord Jesus Christ. It is only a Christian who can suffer exploitation and take it with a smile and express joy! Christ can turn any situation into a profit for Himself. A Christian is to work in honest dedication, for it is primarily a service to the Lord that he gives and Christ is the One who judges in all fairness and justice (see Col. 3:24). The real reward for doing the best you can on the job is the heavenly Father's approval.

The one who does wrong will receive the consequences of the wrong he has done, whether in this life or at the day of judgment (see Rom. 14:10; 2 Cor. 5:10).

See My truth, My child
    I preserved it for you
Search my words and
    You'll see they are true.
Allow them My child
    To fill your whole life
To guide you amid
    The world's problems and strife.

Take time, My child
    And spend it with Me
Then in your life
    Great changes you'll see
Great blessings await you,
    My child, My own,
Don't leave your Bible
    Sitting idle and alone.

—Donna Pace

CHRISTIANS AND THEIR WORLD
COLOSSIANS 4

Before you begin your study this week:
1. Pray and ask God to speak to you through His Holy Spirit each day.
2. Use only your Bible for your answers.
3. Write your answers and the verses you have used.
4. Challenge questions are for those who have the time and wish to do them.
5. Personal questions are to be shared with your study group only if you wish to share.
6. As you study, look for a verse to memorize this week. Write it down, carry it with you, tack it to your bulletin board, tape it to the dashboard of your car. Make a real effort to learn the verse and its reference.

FIRST DAY: Read all of Colossians 4 concentrating on verse 1.

1. Colossians 4:1 tells Christian masters to treat their slaves fairly and justly. This can be applied to how an employer treats his employees. According to this verse, how should a person be treated by their master or employer?

2. Can you think of examples of just and fair practices a Christian employer should apply today to fulfill Colossians 4:1?

3. (Personal) Think about the non-Christian work world. Without mentioning any names, what wrong attitudes and practices are often found in the business world today that conflict with the principles given in Colossians 4:1?

4. Colossians 4:1 reminds us of some of the teaching in the Sermon on the Mount given by the Lord Jesus Christ. How does Matthew 7:12 relate to Colossians 4:1?

5 a. **Challenge:** How do the following verses add to the thoughts in Colossians 4:1? Use your own words to summarize if you wish.

   Ephesians 6:8,9

   Hebrews 13:16

   James 4:17

   b. (Personal) Which of these verses gave you a new thought or challenged you in some way?

6 Read Proverbs 29:20-27 and choose two or three verses that particularly impress you as important principles for employer-employee relationships.

SECOND DAY: Read Colossians 4:2-4.

1. According to Colossians 4:2, what attitude is the Christian to have concerning prayer?

2. a. Perhaps Paul was reminding all Christians to guard against what happened on the Mount of Transfiguration (see Luke 9:32), or he may have been thinking of the Garden of Gethsemane (see Matt. 26:40,41). What do these verses say?

   Luke 9:32

   Matthew 26:40,41

   b. (Personal) Did you find a personal challenge to persevere in prayer in the verses in 2a?

3. a. What does Psalm 5:3 say about prayer?

   b. (Personal) Do you believe that Psalm 5:3 suggests a good way to begin the day? What other times of the day and night have you found to be good times for you to watch and pray?

4. a. **Challenge:** According to Colossians 4:2 we are to pray "with thanks to God." How do the following verses challenge us to be thankful to God?

   Psalm 100:4,5

Romans 12:12

1 Thessalonians 5:18

   b. (Personal) Was one of these verses a special help to you in your present circumstances? Are you able to verbally express your thoughts on thankfulness to God and the rewards of peace and patience it has brought into your life?

5 a. We are also to pray with thanksgiving before our meals. We should be especially conscious of the blessing of food God has given to us, as many people in our world are starving to death. How does Mark 8:6,7 describe how the Lord Jesus Christ set a pattern for prayer before eating food?

   b. (Personal) Do you believe that prayer before eating your food can be a witness of your faith in Christ? Are there ever occasions when you feel that prayer should be omitted?

6. a. What does Paul ask the Christians to pray for in Colossians 4:3,4?

   b. Christians should pray faithfully for their ministers, missionaries, Bible teachers and Sunday School teachers. How do the following verses remind you to pray for these people?

   Romans 10:14

2 Corinthians 2:14,17

THIRD DAY: Read Colossians 4:5,6.

1. What does Colossians 4:5,6 say? Try putting the thoughts into your own words if you wish and insert your name to personalize these verses.

2. **Challenge:** Christians are to redeem the time or make good use of every opportunity God gives according to Colossians 4:5. How do the following verses make you think about the use of your time?

   Psalm 90:12

   Ephesians 5:15-17

   James 4:14,15

3. (Personal) Is there some change you feel God is leading you to make in your value system and use of time?

4. Our speech is to be "seasoned with salt" or never insipid (see Col. 4:6) when we speak of our faith in the Lord Jesus Christ. How do these verses help you to understand and also learn to speak this way?

   Mark 9:50

   1 Peter 3:15

141

5. The words in Colossians 4:5, "them that are without," or those who are not believers, refers to those people who have not yet placed their faith in Jesus Christ as their Lord and Savior. In Ezekiel 18:32 what do you learn concerning God's love and longing to have these people turn to Him in faith?

6 a. How do the following verses reveal the life available through faith in Jesus Christ?

Acts 4:12

Romans 5:1

b. (Personal) Have you ever chosen to receive Christ into your life? (see Matt. 1:21; Rom. 10:9,10).

FOURTH AND FIFTH DAYS: Read Colossians 4:7-18.

1 a. Paul mentioned all of the men who were with him in Rome. How is Tychicus described and why did Paul send him to Colosse?

b. What similar task did Paul give to Tychicus concerning the Ephesian Christians? (see Eph. 6:21,22).

c. Who was to go along with Tychicus? Give verse please.

2 a. **Challenge:** Read Acts 13:5,13 with Acts 12:12, which give

you background on John Mark. Briefly describe who John Mark was and what he did in Acts 13:13.

    b. How does Paul say the Colossian Christians should receive John Mark, sometimes translated Marcus, sister's son to Barnabas?

3 a. Who was another man who had been a comfort to Paul and a fellowworker in the kingdom of God? (see Col. 4:11).

    b. What was Epaphras, a servant of Christ, doing for the Colossian Christians while he was in Rome?

    c. (Personal) Do you pray for people as Epaphras did? Do you believe God wants you to make a prayer list and begin to earnestly pray for those you know?

4. What two other people were in Rome with Paul and sent their greetings to the Colossian Christians?

5 a. All of these men must have given comfort and encouragement to Paul as he was a prisoner in Rome. Today we as Christians are to comfort, help and pray for each other, too. How do the following verses express this Christian duty and privilege?

John 13:35

James 2:15-17

1 John 3:17

b. (Personal) Which verse meant the most to you? Why?

6. Review the verse in this lesson that you memorized this week. Write the verse and its address and keep it along with others you have learned in an accessible place so you can easily review your verses and grow in your spiritual treasure chest.

SIXTH DAY: Read all the Notes and look up the Scriptures.

1. What new thought did you find helpful in the Notes?

2. What personal application did you select to apply to your own life this week?

Study Notes

It appears that Colossians 4:1 refers back to Colossians 3:22-25. "Remember, then, you employers to be fair and just toward those whom you employ, never forgetting that you yourselves have a heavenly Employer" (*Phillips*). Many translations use the word *slave-owners* and *slaves* or *masters* and *servants* in place of the words *employers* and *employee*.

God's Master Plan on the Job Colossians 4:1

Slavery was practiced in Paul's day, but today we can relate these same principles to men and women in the business world. In Colossians 4:1 the employee is to be treated justly and equally, or as the *New International Version* puts it, "right and fair."

Certainly a Christian employer should never forget that he has a heavenly Employer, the Lord Jesus Christ, and therefore should practice Christ's just and fair practices in his own business relationships with his employees! He should give "fair" wages, expect a "fair" amount of work, set "fair" hours, have "fair" health plans, and have "fair" working conditions, "fair" rest periods as well as "fair" vacations!

In the non-Christian working world, there are many wrong attitudes and practices that are contrary to God's master plan. We often hear of the man who is soon to retire with a fair retirement salary being fired just one or two years before he is to receive his "fair and justly" earned retirement. Such practices are wrong, not only in the sight of man, but in the sight of God. This reminds us of the verse in the Sermon on the Mount which says, "Do for others what you want them to do for you" (Matt. 7:12, *TLB*). Each of us should ask, If I were an employee, how would I want to be treated? It is then that the employer will treat his employee in a right and fair way. "Therefore to him that knoweth to do good, and doeth it not, to him it is sin" (Jas. 4:17, *KJV*; see also 1 Tim. 6:17,18; Eph. 6:8,9; Prov. 29:20-27).

The Christian employee and employer all work for the glory of God so that men, women and children may have the things they need for living. The employer must remember that just as his workers, he is answerable to God. Every Christian should realize that his business belongs to God and God has only put him in charge of it!

Prayer Is a Privilege Colossians 4:2-4

In this next section Paul, as led by the Holy Spirit, wrote to encourage all Christians to participate in the great privilege of prayer. "Don't be weary in prayer; keep at it; watch for God's answers and remember to be thankful when they come" (Col. 4:2, *TLB*).

Sometimes when we pray it seems our prayers go no higher than the ceiling. At such a time the remedy for this emotion is not to stop praying but to go on praying! We are to keep at it, for a person who prays will discover that "spiritual dryness will not last! Prayerless work will soon slacken and never fruit" (McLaren). The great preacher, Moody, used to quote a man—Williams—by saying, "Our prayers often resemble the mischievous tricks of town children, who knock at their neighbor's houses and then run away; we often knock at heaven's door and then run off." Moody would go on to quote Williams in this way, "Instead of waiting for entrance and answer, we act as if we were afraid of having a prayer answered."

In her book *Hotline to Heaven,* F. Gardner gives an illustration of symbolically taking our requests to God and believing that He will answer our prayers, in His perfect timing. Her instructions are:

One. Put your hand symbolically out toward God.

Two. Straighten out your arm and reach out as far as you possibly can. This will make sure that your hand is as far from yourself as you can physically make it.

Three. Turn your palm so that it is right side up.

Four. Now in your hand, with the palm turned up, give God the prayer request on your heart. What are you going to do with your hand? You have a choice of two things. You can either clench your hand and return your prayer burden to your own heart, or you can very simply follow the next step.

Five. Simply turn your hand upside down so that nothing can possibly stay in your hand. Make sure that your fist isn't clenched to hold something, but stretch your fingers as far apart as possible.

Six. Drop your arm to your side.

In this way, as you pray, you can't bring back anything you have given to God! This is the only way to pray. Oftentimes we go to God with our requests, and then carry our prayer burdens right back into our own hearts. Sometimes we even make the attempt to answer our own prayers! By faith we need to trust Him to answer our prayers. "Therefore I tell you, whatever you ask for in prayer, believe that you have received it, and it will be yours. And when you stand praying, if you hold anything against anyone, forgive him, so that your Father in heaven may forgive you your sins" (Mark 11:24,25, *NIV*). The Lord Jesus also said this about prayer in John 14:13,14: "Whatever you ask in My name, that will I do, that the Father may be glorified in the Son. If you ask Me anything in My name, I will do it" (*NASB*).

Listen for God's Answers

One of the most important things in prayer is to wait to hear what God has to say to you! Many times we pray, feeling God is not going to do anything about our problem. So we take our problem back and try to solve it on our own. Many times we run about asking everyone's advice, then have not the time to remain still long enough to discover what God wants to say. Part of the secret of prayer then is to take time to listen to God's answers.

But don't expect an audible voice to give you complete instructions! God will give you instructions, but you need to know how to recognize His answers to you. Ask God to reveal them to you, and many times answers will come through other people or through reading His Word. The Scripture is a personal letter written to you, and the Holy Spirit will point out what God wants to reveal in His plan; He will answer your prayers as you read and study God's Word.

Why doesn't God always answer our prayers the way we think they should be answered? God knows what's best for us, and whatever He has planned is far better than what we could plan! So if you get an answer from God that's not quite what you expected, remember that God knows the needs of your life better than you do, and that's why He is answering His way!

Make a Record of Your Prayers

It's exciting to keep a prayer notebook! You can list your praise and worship to God for answers to prayer, for His love and forgiveness. Include a request section where you list family, church, missionary, neighbors' and friends' needs. Have a column to date when you made requests to God and then have a praise column where you can put the date of the answer or partial answer to prayer. It's a good idea to make a new notebook each year, but be sure to save the old one in memory of what God has done for you!

It does take an act of the will to spend time each day in prayer. Emotions keep pulling us the other way. It may be a struggle all the way through your first prayer time, but remember that you will have a good time if you continue a daily prayer. Eventually, as J. Sidlow Baxter puts it, "The whole intellect, will and emotions will be united in one coordinated operation. It is then that God becomes real, heaven is open, and prayer becomes surprisingly vital!" God has been watching and listening through your days of struggle, chilling moods and multitudinous emotions, even if you haven't felt it yourself!

Prayer—A Christian's Supreme Power and Strategy

In the holy war, which we Christians are called to wage against the powers of evil, prayer is our supreme power and strategy. Through prayer we get to know our risen Lord Jesus in a close and developing friendship. At last, when we meet Him in heaven, we shall look into His dear face and find ourselves saying, "At last I have seen face to face the one whom for years I have known heart-to-heart."

We are instructed to "watch for God's answers and remember to be thankful when they come" (Col. 4:2, *TLB*). A similar thought is given in many portions of Scripture. We are to pray constantly and give thanks to God for the answers. Some people feel that prayer has to come only at certain times. As we learn to depend more and more on God, we realize that we can pray at any time and in any place! We can pray while walking about our house, driving a car, or even while having a conversation with someone—asking God to give direction in the conversation. We are to pray for everything, asking wisdom at all times!

When someone gives you a prayer request, stop right where you are, whether you are with them in person or on the telephone, and pray right at that very moment, asking God to lead and guide you in the situation, and commit whatever the problem is to Him. And then "watch for God's answers and remember to be thankful when they come."

"[Pray] at the same time for us as well, that God may open up to us a door for the word, so that we may speak forth the mystery of Christ, for which I have also been imprisoned; in order that I may make it clear in the way I ought to speak" (Col. 4:3,4, *NASB*). Here Paul asked for prayer for himself to be able to share the good news about the Lord Jesus Christ both boldly and plainly even while he was in jail! He was not so much asking for prayer for himself but prayer for his work in sharing Jesus Christ.

Paul might have asked that they pray for his release from prison, or for a little rest and peace at the last, but he only asked that they pray he be given strength and opportunity to do the work for which God had sent him into the world. We need to pray this way for ourselves and for others—that we might complete the task assigned to us in this world. Paul's prayer was for power—not for release! "Likewise the Spirit helps us in our weakness; for we do not know how to pray as we ought, but the Spirit himself intercedes for us with sighs too deep for words. And he who searches the hearts of men knows what is the mind of the Spirit, because the Spirit intercedes for the saints according to the will of God. We know that in everything God works for good with those who love him, who are called according to his purpose" (Rom. 8:26-28, *RSV*).

The Christian and the World Colossians 4:5,6

In this section the Holy Spirit led Paul to speak about the outward life of a Christian. We found in earlier chapters of Colossians that we build within, cultivating the virtues of the new life in Christ (see Col. 2:6-10; 3:3,12). We must cultivate the virtues of our new life in Christ, but there is something more! We want our new life to be seen and felt among others (see Col. 4:5). This is the way we present Christ to the world. Remember, the term *Christian* means "little Christ." Christ is living in us! His life is told today in the "living letters" that are known and read of all men—the living letters are the lives of Christians.

> ***Christians must live in wisdom and use tact as they meet those outside the church.***

"Behave wisely towards those outside your own number; use the present opportunity to the full. Let your conversation be always gracious and never insipid; study how best to talk with each person you meet" (Col. 4:5,6, *NEB*). "Make the most of your chances to tell others the Good News. Be wise in all your contacts with them. Let your conversation be gracious as well as sensible, for then you will have the right answer for everyone" (Col. 4:5,6, *TLB*). It is good to compare these different translations with the *King James Version* of this passage as we discover certain new insights from each version.

Christians must live in wisdom and use tact as they meet those outside the church, and all Christians, according to this passage, are missionaries or ambassadors for Jesus Christ. "For God was in Christ, restoring the world to himself, no longer counting men's sins against them but blotting them out. This is the wonderful message he has given us to tell others. We are Christ's ambassadors. God is using us to speak to you: we beg you, as though Christ himself were here pleading with you, receive the love he offers you—be reconciled to God. For God took the sinless Christ and poured into him our sins. Then, in exchange, he poured God's goodness into us!" (2 Cor. 5:19-

21, *TLB*). If you never have allowed God to "exchange your sins for Christ's goodness," after reading this passage won't you consider inviting God to do this for you? "Right now God is ready to welcome you. Today he is ready to save you" (2 Cor. 6:2, *TLB*).

The *King James Version* of Colossians 4:6 reads: "Let your speech be alway with grace, seasoned with salt, that ye may know how ye ought to answer every man." Someone has calculated that each person utters some 30,000 words each day! If these words were put into print they would amount to a very large book. These books would, in a lifetime, fill a college library! Yes, you are an author, whether you realize it or not! Everything you say and do reflects your inner thoughts and motives. What a responsibility we have to follow the advice in Colossians 4:6: "Let your conversation be gracious as well as sensible, for then you will have the right answer for everyone" (*TLB*). How thankful a Christian can be that the penalty of misspoken words, evil thoughts, and unconsecrated deeds can be covered by the blood of Christ (see 1 John 1:8,9).

> You are writing each day a letter to men,
> Take care that the writing is true,
> It's the only Gospel that some men will read,
> The Gospel according to you!
> —Anonymous

There is an old saying, "What is in the well of your heart is bound to come up in the bucket of your speech!" (Bieber).

Complete Your Work in the Lord Colossians 4:7-18

In Colossians 4:10-14, Paul spoke of his co-workers who had ministered and been fellow servants in the Lord, some of whom he sent to the Colossian church to tell about his own circumstances and to encourage these Christians' hearts. He named each man—Tychicus, Onesimus, Aristarchus, Marcus (known as Mark, the writer of the Gospel), Justus, Epaphras, Luke, the beloved physician and Demas.

After giving a brief description of each one of these men and their encouragement, Paul sent greetings to the Laodicean church and to the house church of Nymphas. He requested that his letter be read to the Laodiceans. Laodicea was about 10 miles downstream from the Colossian churches. He also requested that his letter to the Laodiceans be read to the Colossian churches. Nothing is known about it except that it was lost. Paul must have written many other letters, which we do not have today. After dictating the letter, Paul confirmed its genuineness as was his custom by referring to his "bonds" and signing it personally with his own hand. "He who is suffering on behalf of Christ has a right to speak on behalf of Christ" (Lightfoot). On this moving note Paul closed his letter.

Colossians 4:17 contains a message for Archippus. "And say to Archippus, 'See that you fulfil the ministry which you have received in the Lord'" (*RSV*). When Epaphras departed from Colosse to visit Paul in Rome, someone had to be left in charge. Since this was a public letter read before the church, the phrase would have its own personal meaning to Archippus. Armed with its authority, the letter of Colossians could have amounted to credentials, signifying he was the one to lead the faithful Christians away from false teachers. With Epaphras still in prison with Paul, unable to return to his church and act as their official minister, the task appeared to have fallen on Archippus. If this was true, he would understand the phrase to mean, "You're the only one there I can count on to protect the people from false teachers. It would be disastrous for them if you fail to accept your responsibility."

> ***The place that Christ holds in any religious teaching determines whether it is true or false.***

Heresy had broken out in the church at Colosse, misleading the young believers, calling for the worship of angels (see Col. 2:18) and a strict observance of Jewish ceremonies (see Col. 2:16-21). This heresy was a mixture of Jewish, Greek and Oriental religions. Colossians reproves the heresy with the statement of the supreme Lordship of Christ. This Epistle draws a faithful portrait of Christ in all His glory and dignity. The place that Christ holds in any religious teaching determines whether it is true or false.

Some taught in Paul's day, as now, that Jesus was but a man and Christ was the divine Spirit, which came at Jesus' baptism and left Him at the cross. This meant simply that Jesus, not Christ, died. You can see that this is the root of error of many false teachings today. It's good for us, in studying the Colossian letter, to examine our own beliefs and see that we always put the Head, Christ Jesus, in His rightful place in our thinking. "Unto you is born this day in the city of David a Saviour, which is Christ the Lord" (Luke 2:11, *KJV*). "God also hath highly exalted him, and given him a name which is above every name: that at the name of Jesus every knee should bow, of things in heaven, and things in earth, and things under the earth, and that every tongue should confess that Jesus Christ is Lord, to the glory of God the Father" (Phil. 2:9-11, *KJV*).

> Oh happy day that fixed my choice
> On Thee, my Saviour and my God!
> Well may this glowing heart rejoice,
> And tell its raptures all abroad.
> Happy day, happy day,
> When Jesus washed my sins away!
> He taught me how to watch and pray,
> And live rejoicing ev'ry day.
> —Philip Doddridge (1702-1751)

"He who most clearly discerns the perfect character of Jesus will be most urgent in prayer for grace to grow like Him" (C.H. Spurgeon).

> The Power House
> Is always there,
> So push the button,
> Labeled "Prayer."
>
> —Ralph H. Dumont

The Joy of Living Series...

COURAGE TO CONQUER
Studies in Daniel
DORIS W. GREIG

An in-depth look at a companion of kings, leader of men and a man truly devoted to his God. Today's world can learn from his uncompromising example. A 6-week study. **5419489**

WALKING IN GOD'S WAY
Studies in Ruth and Esther
RUTH BATHAUER & DORIS W. GREIG

A 7-week study. Learn about God's special love for us and how He is leading our every step. Explore how circumstances never stand in the way of God's perfect plan for our lives. **5419474**

LIVING IN THE LIGHT
Studies in 1, 2 and 3 John, and Jude
DORIS W. GREIG

This 6-week study focuses on the fundamentals of Christianity, exploring the sovereignty of Christ and how we as Christians should live in the glorious light of His love. **5419501**

POWER FOR POSITIVE LIVING
Studies in Philippians and Colossians
DORIS W. GREIG

This study focuses on the Christian life of joy and hope as expressed in Philippians and Colossians. We can be joyful, even in a world of sorrow, and resist the powers of evil if we stand fast in the knowledge of our Lord. **5419493**

Other Joy of Living Bible Studies are available at your local Christian bookstore.

Joy of Living for Larger Community Bible Study and Fellowship Groups

Nine 28-Lesson Courses to Choose From

The Joy of Living Bible Study Inc., founded by Doris W. Greig, started publishing for group use in the early 1970s. Since that time 9 courses written by Doris Greig, Ruth Bathauer and Jean W. Randall, of 28 lessons each, have been published and are available from the Joy of Living office in Glendale, Calif.

These lessons are provided in an 8½" × 11" page format, 8 pages per weekly lesson, including 4 pages of Bible commentary and application notes for the prior week's study. In addition there are 4 pages of daily, personal Bible study questions for sharing in the following week's group discussion.

Joy of Living classes usually meet once a week. Individuals are encouraged to study privately using the questions and commentary they receive in class. This material is an excellent guide for daily Bible study as participants write their answers to the questions.

At the weekly meeting participants have opportunity to meet in small groups to discuss their answers and to pray together. Following this, the small groups may join together for a brief lecture by the Joy of Living teaching leader. As members leave, they are given the 4 pages of Bible commentary notes plus the 4 pages of personal Bible Study questions for the following week's study. Each weekly set of commentary and daily study questions is available separately.

For samples, full information, or a listing of Joy of Living classes in your area, write or phone:

Joy of Living Bible Studies
Box 129, Glendale, CA 91209
818/244-2665